Remembering The Ladies

Remembering The Ladies

ANN COVELL

Outskirts Press, Inc.
Denver, Colorado

Outskirts Press, Inc.
http://www.outskirtspress.com

ISBN: 978-1-4327-5402-0

Library of Congress Control Number: 2010921337

Outskirts Press and the "OP" logo are trademarks belonging to Outskirts Press, Inc.

PRINTED IN THE UNITED STATES OF AMERICA

This book is for

JOHN ENGLAND COVELL

my husband, my mentor, my rock

Also for my beautiful step-granddaughters

Sally Barrett

Rebecca Covell and Lucy Covell

Hannah Parkhouse and Laura Parkhouse

Acknowledgements

Writing a book is time-consuming, and with an already-busy life, my friends wondered how I would be able to do it. I would not have been able to do so without the help I received from the following:

The Methodist Church in Chelston, Devonshire, for the use of their Choir Vestry during the early research days, providing me with a peaceful, quiet study area.

The gracious staff at the Mijas Hotel in Mijas Pueblo, Costa del Sol, Spain, who left me alone in a peaceful corner with a beautiful view and wonderful coffee, as I wrestled daily with the problem of putting dozens of facts into one small paragraph.

Martha Regula and staff at the National First Ladies Library in Canton, Ohio, for arranging my visit to them and for their wisdom and support in my quest for information on the nineteenth-century First Ladies.

Graphic Artist, Angus Elton-Miller, for his design and artwork of the front-cover and the internal illustrations.

Richard Meek, for his sustained and essential IT support

Larry Morando of Outskirts Press, who quietly gave me tremendous support.

My eleven-year-old step-granddaughter, Hannah Parkhouse (an aspiring writer herself,) whose interest and encouragement rallied me when, at a low ebb, I almost gave up the project.

Last but not least, my husband, John, for his patience, consideration, and ability to hearten me. He made all the difference in the world.

Contents

Introduction

Michelle Obama had already secured a place in history when she became the first Black First Lady of America in January 2009. A few weeks later, while travelling with President Barack Obama who was attending a major international conference in London, she established another historical milestone. In an incident that may endure in Britain's memory, Queen Elizabeth broke with convention when she slipped an arm around the First Lady. Used to the sedate aloofness of royal protocol which dictates that the Sovereign is never to touch, or be touched, by another in public, observers watched in astonishment as Mrs. Obama gently returned the gesture. There appeared to be a mutual liking and respect between the two powerful women, and it delighted everyone. This was a far cry from the Royal Court's haughty frostiness toward John Adams and his wife, Abigail, when John became the first American ambassador to the Court of St. James (1785–1788).

The charm and warmth exuding from Mrs. Obama's

meeting with the Queen was reflected throughout her stay in Europe, as everyone wanted to be near her. She was portrayed in the media as a stylish, elegant woman who is true to herself, modern, self-assured, realistic, full of common sense and sensitivity, and a doting wife and mother. It was obvious to onlookers that she would fulfil her uniquely American role with the same poise and confidence of many of her predecessors.

Soon after Barack Obama's election in November 2008, he responded to media questions about his wife, indicating that she would design her own role and set her own path. Although the role of the First Lady has never been fully defined within the American Constitution, this sentiment could be attributed to a number of twentieth-century First Ladies. As that century progressed, opportunities developed for them that the nineteenth-century presidencies had neither allowed nor contemplated. In the recent past, the world has witnessed a former First Lady, Hillary Rodham Clinton, become a powerful senator, a formidable candidate for the presidential nomination, and appointed as secretary of state. No one can comment upon Mrs. Clinton without applauding her ambitions and achievements since she first entered the White House in 1993. As her political ambitions surfaced, it became apparent she might somehow transform the role of First Lady. A number of her predecessors had ventured to do this, either by design or providence.

As early as 1901, when Theodore Roosevelt became the twenty-sixth president, his wife, Edith Kermit Carow Roosevelt, became an impressive force within the White

House, as did succeeding First Ladies, Helen Herron Taft,
Ellen Axson Wilson (first wife of President Woodrow
Wilson), and Edith Bolling Galt Wilson (Wilson's second
wife). Edith Roosevelt oozed confidence and self-assurance
as she began quietly to make changes that others may never
have risked. Within eight years, she had separated the president's personal apartments from his official rooms. In order
to control a voracious public insistence for personal details,
she arranged for periodic posed photographs and anecdotes
about the presidential family to be forwarded to the press. She
began a weekly meeting with the wives of cabinet members
in an effort to establish financial boundaries for individual
departmental receptions, thus avoiding situations when one
event might be judged inferior to another. She relinquished
the planning of formal entertaining by hiring specialty ca-
terers, and she introduced a secretariat to deal with her official correspondence. No one since Elizabeth Monroe, wife
of President James Monroe (1817–1825), had, at that time,
influenced the First Lady role so radically.

Helen Herron Taft, wife of President William Taft (1909–
1913), had neither the quiet self-restraint nor the enterprise
of Mrs. Roosevelt, but her purism and ambition were strong
motivators. In spite of serious illness, she exuded a strong
presence in the White House. Born in an era when wom-
en were able to achieve limited personal prominence, she
chose to achieve long-held political ambitions through her
husband's career. When William became governor of the
Philippines, she strove for perfection. Later, she encouraged
her unwilling husband to run for the presidency and she set

a precedent by riding back to the White House with him following his inauguration ceremony. Traditionally, as the retir-
ing president, Roosevelt would have returned with the new
president, but he had decided to leave Washington prior to
the inauguration. Mrs. Taft claimed the privilege, publicly
signalling an intention to play an important part in her husband's administration. For the next two months, she helped
and encouraged the reluctant, ill-at-ease president, but her
determination to shield him from the stresses of his job
led to her own decline in health, and she suffered a stroke.
The ambitious First Lady was forced into relying on family
members to substitute for her at receptions and other events,
causing her much anguish. As she recovered, however, she
became successful in introducing revolutionary economies
within the White House. She appointed a lower-paid female
housekeeper (Elizabeth Jaffray), rather than a male steward,
and ordered a continuous scrutiny of all expenditures. As a
result of her strict budget regulations, she amassed savings
of $80,000 by the end of the Taft presidency in 1913, a sig-
nificant achievement.

Woodrow Wilson's presidency (1913-21) saw the lift-
ing of many political barriers against women. Jane Addams
had already astonished the population when she publicly
nominated Theodore Roosevelt for president. It was equally surprising when Montana's Jeanette Rankin became the
first woman to take a seat in the House of Representatives in
1917, and when the Nineteenth Amendment was ratified in
1920, giving the majority of women the same voting rights
as men. As a reluctant supporter of suffrage, Wilson accepted

the amendment as inevitable.

Born into a strong background when men fully controlled their households, Wilson preferred compliant women though his first wife, Ellen Axson, did not fulfil that predilection. As a well educated woman and a convincing artist with a streak of independence, she was averse to her husband's prejudice against intelligent women and his disappointment that she bore him three daughters but no son. She had relinquished her art career when she married, concentrating instead on encouraging her husband in his political career. However, when he was appointed governor of New Jersey, it was Ellen who received press attention when some of her artwork were published nationally. She eschewed the political scene whenever she could, though there was an incident in 1911 when she allegedly set up a meeting with William Jennings Bryant, an eminent Democrat. This led Bryant to support and help during the 1912 Democrat nomination race, which Wilson won.

Ellen concentrated her efforts on improving slum housing conditions, particularly for the Black population. Under her influence, slum clearance became a worthy, urgent subject for discussion. In February 1914, legislation known as "Ellen Wilson's Bill" was introduced in Congress. The bill remained in a congressional committee awaiting a decision on the funding for the necessary improvements for quite a while. When Ellen lay terminally ill from a kidney disease, the House of Representatives quickly approved the measure so that she could be told of their decision before her death. That was the first time important legislation had been passed with such direct mediation from a First Lady, and following her death in August 1914, newspaper obituaries acknowledged her unique place in history. Had she been the First Lady a few decades earlier, it would have been unthinkable for her to be allowed to visit the slum areas, let alone influence such an important bill.

President Wilson married Edith Bolling Galt in December 1915, just as the Women's Suffrage movement had become a force to be reckoned with. A Quaker, Alice Paul, had formed a group of prominent suffragists who hoped to bring about Wilson's defeat through the nine states already given suffrage, and especially from Illinois, where women were allowed to vote in presidential elections. Wilson was elected to his second term in 1916 by a slim majority, and he realised the power of women was no longer of minor importance. Edith never showed interest in the suffrage movement due to her concern that it might affect her husband's health negatively. She was probably relieved when many suffragists turned their energies to the war effort when America entered the Great War in 1917.

Edith was well received in Europe in November 1918 when President Wilson travelled there to liaise on the European Peace Treaty details, though her prominent position in American history was not established until the following year when her husband suffered a paralytic stroke. Wilson's physician refused to comment on the illness, and the president's condition remained uncertain for several weeks. The devastated First Lady had fully agreed with the physician's recommendation that all presidential matters should be kept from her husband until he was considered fit enough to cope with them.

There was considerable uncertainty as to when and to whom the presidential duties should be passed. No precedent had been set about a temporary "takeover" of presidential duties, and since the Constitution was imprecise on the issue, the matter remained in abeyance, pending further advice from the physician. Wilson was isolated from administrative staff for a number of weeks, and the First Lady screened any communications that did reach him. It was not long before suspicions arose that Edith was making presidential decisions, especially when signed documents appeared to have forged signatures. Edith countered these speculations by stating that her husband's paralysis had affected his handwriting and that he was gradually improving. Rumours persisted, however, that Edith Wilson was running a "petticoat" government, and, as she appeared to have control over access to the president, a number of requests began to be addressed directly to her. The worried cabinet again considered the procedure to follow when a president was seriously incapacitated but refused to relinquish office.

The only precedent concerning the health of a president was that of President Garfield's three-month illness following an assassination attempt in 1881. Garfield's vice president, Chester Arthur, had not taken over the president's duties on a temporary basis, just as Vice President Thomas R. Marshall had not taken over any of Wilson's presidential responsibilities. In their dilemma, the cabinet agreed that Senator Albert Fall (New Mexico) should visit the president in order to ascertain and report back on his current condition. By that time, however, the president's strength had improved, and he was able to shake Fall's hand and sign documents from his bed in his presence. After receiving the senator's feedback, the cabinet decided once more to hold all decisions in abeyance. Wilson recovered sufficiently well to fulfil the rest of his term.

However, the so-called petticoat government had demonstrated a weakness within the Constitution, as the wife of a president had had the power to decide his fitness to preside over the nation. Edith Wilson is recorded in American history as being the first president's wife to dominate the presidency during difficult times, and many citizens were alarmed at the potential power in the First Lady's role. The Twenty-fifth Amendment, which rectified this constitutional anomaly, was passed in 1967.

The attainments of these four "new-century" women cannot be compared to the frustrations of predecessors such as Abigail Adams (1797–1801) and Sarah Polk (1845–49), who, almost half a century apart, shared an intense propensity to improve the lives of American women. Their undisguised ambitions were never launched, the timing of their tenure making all the difference. Education, or lack of it, played a large part in the Adams' struggle. She fought without success for improved schooling for girls and equal legal rights for women over property and children. By the middle of the nineteenth century, a number of schools and colleges for females had been founded, and the intellectual Sarah Polk had received an intensive education. Her scholastic efforts were often impeded, however, by the lack of legal rights for women that continued to burden the female sex within her century.

The First Ladies of the nineteenth century were a mixed group consisting of wives, daughters, daughters-in-law, sisters, and friends ranging in age from the early twenties to the late sixties. A number of the women who had served in the latter half of the century had, in fact, benefited from intense tutoring (Sarah Polk, Harriet Lane, Lucy Hayes, Frances Cleveland), though the majority received only trivial tutoring in basic arithmetic, reading, and writing—sufficient to allow them to manage a household. Some had shown extreme courage either prior to or during the presidency (Dolley Madison, Louisa Adams, Elizabeth Monroe); some had a sense of adventure (Harriet Lane, Margaret Taylor, Abigail Fillmore); while others never actually assumed the full role of First Lady. There were those who appeared emotionally unstable (Jane Pierce, Mary Lincoln), whose sad lives were misunderstood by the nation.

Few of these women came under the same blazing spotlights of the nation as in this modern age, though they all suffered the glare of publicity within the tight socialite community of the capital city, often enduring the experience of insidious misrepresentation. In an era with few national newspapers and journals, and with photography in its infancy, it was the president whose picture hung in towns and cities throughout the land and who would visit the various states. The First Lady was rarely seen outside the capital and remained almost unknown to the nation's citizens until the latter part of the century.

The essays within this book provide a brief insight into the compelling lives of the nineteenth-century First Ladies, who often suffered formidable adversities. They were undeniably women of character, as were all of the women linked to the first hundred years of the American presidency.

Phase One

BUILDING THE FOUNDATIONS

1789-1829

Martha Washington

Abigail Adams

The Jefferson Ladies

Dolley Madison

Elizabeth Monroe

Louisa Adams

Building The Foundations

George Washington's wife, Martha, was launched head-first into the role of First Lady, with neither preparation nor guidance. She was expected to represent an idealized image of American womanhood, and for a woman in her sixties, yearning to live a quiet, rural life with her husband, it was an oppressive task from day one.

Americans were aware of the powerful, prominent women of Europe's royal houses, but they did not perceive Mrs. Washington's new role in that context, nor did they wish it. Indeed, the cries of affection and waving of flags reported in the newspapers, as she travelled to the seat of the new nation in New York, appeared to honour "Lady Washington," wife of the famous General Washington, rather than the wife of the president of the United States. The population did not see much more of Martha Washington after that journey, sometimes catching glimpses of her as she travelled within New York (and later Philadelphia), or at her "Drawing Room" receptions.

Many believed that Martha's form of greeting at her social events, seated as she was on a slightly raised platform, implied a formal royal court reception. This seemed appropriate only to the Federalists, some of whom suggested that George Washington should become king and that his wife should be treated with "royal" deference. George Washington did not agree and the anti-Federalist secretary of state, Thomas Jefferson, championed his stance. Jefferson, writer of the original draft of the Declaration of Independence, was vociferous in his condemnation of the veneration which began to be showered upon Martha. A great debate ensued about the titles which the president and his wife should be known by, and the ideas of royal titles and personas were dispelled quickly. Martha continued to be known as "Lady Washington," the affectionate title given to her during the war years by adoring soldiers, and the use of "Lady" continued during the tenures of Adams and Madison. It would be almost nine decades, however, before "First Lady" became the recognised form of address.

Foundations for much of the twofold presidential role as head of government and head of state had been established by the time George Washington had completed his two terms. Martha Washington had no role to play in her husband's responsibility as head of government, and there is no evidence that she ever attempted to do so, or that her husband ever sought her opinion.

As head of state, it was always assumed that the president would enlist his wife's help in ceremonial and similar duties. Martha willingly carried out this function, helping the president to present as an egalitarian, eager to please the public. George Washington, an imposing man of well over six feet in height, had a somewhat magisterial bearing and a powerful aura surrounded him as he entered a room. Therefore, it was not difficult to attract the awe and deference his office justified. On the occasions when it was not appropriate, however, Martha kept the balance by her unassuming, gentle manner, avoiding needless criticism of her husband's austere demeanour. Such criticism came often, though the president could never understand this or why conversations were so difficult at his wife's weekly Drawing Room events when he tried to get tongue-tied ladies to respond to his trivial chat. Martha attended most social events with the president, even attending on his behalf if he were too busy (or tired). Her solo visits to families of cabinet members and official visitors were well received, and, in the absence of the president for any reason, she offered her courteous attention to all visitors to the presidential home. She also undertook the task of organizing official receptions and dinners while controlling the smooth running of the presidential home.

This meek, likeable lady, who had established her parameters within the limits of domesticity, became renowned as the quintessential hostess model of the era. Thus, she set the precedent for her successors.

When John Adams was inaugurated as the second president, his wife, Abigail, fully maintained the social protocol Martha Washington had established. Another irreproachable model of domestic virtues, she was nevertheless an assertive woman, having been left to manage the farm and bring up four children alone while her husband built a political career in Philadelphia. Her demeanour as the president's wife was not the meek one of her predecessor, especially following copious correspondence with her philosophical husband throughout his long absences. As a result of exchanging thoughts and hopes for the country through their letters, she became comfortable expressing her opinions.

It was obvious that John Adams admired his wife's strengths and powers of deduction and respected her judgement and guidance, though he may often have wished that he could control her sharp, critical tongue, which did nothing to endear her to his political acquaintances. If anyone criticised her husband, she defended him vehemently and gained the title, used disdainfully, of "Mrs. President," within government departments. It was not long before she was accused of playing politics as she continued to advise her husband (informally) on various issues.

When Abigail spoke openly about the widening split between the Republicans and Federalists, Albert Gallatin, one of Adams' opponents, became offended by her outspoken interference and loudly declared his disapproval. Abigail had not noticed she was overstepping the mark, and she continued to assist the president wherever possible, even helping him with the initial drafts of official letters. The public appeared aware of her influence over the president, and some folks requiring presidential approval on an issue would often seek an audience with Abigail in the first instance, though she always refused such requests.

Gallatin and his followers continued to vocalise strong disapproval of Abigail, and his constant rebukes may well have soured voters and members of the cabinet against her. This, together with Thomas Jefferson's estrangement from his former friend on political issues, particularly the Alien and Sedition Acts, had detrimental effects on the result of the 1800 election campaign, which Adams lost.

Abigail had not effected any significant change in the role of the president's wife, but one could ponder on what might have been achieved had John Adams gained a second term. However, her tenure demonstrated that interference from an unelected person, even the president's wife as his closest companion, would not be tolerated.

So, within a dozen years of the new presidential system, there were two conflicting examples of presidential "wifely" behaviour. While it was obvious that Martha Washington's style was the one of preference, a question posed then could have asked which particular model would eventually dominate. In the mood of that era, the answer may well have been that should a presidential consort intrude into government issues in the future, there would always be a "Gallatin" figure ready to criticise!

That question, however, was not asked during the two terms served by widower Thomas Jefferson (1801–1809). He believed strongly that a spouse or lady was unimportant in the household, especially following the experience of Abigail Adams' alleged intrusions. He decided he could run the presidential house himself, with the help of staff, for was he not an excellent chef and sommelier himself? He did not endorse the pomp and circumstance of presidential functions and allowed a disorderly arrangement of seating at official dinners and receptions, an unpopular innovation, and withdrew the Friday evening Drawing Room receptions. Eventually, he had to concede that the presence of a hostess when women were expected to attend a dinner party or reception was essential. Undoubtedly, it would have been easier if Jefferson had been able to enlist the help of his vice president's wife. However, Aaron Burr was also a widower, so the president had no option but to call on his elder daughter to undertake a number of formal duties.

Martha Jefferson Randolph rallied to her father's call, though her own home commitments and growing family meant she could not be at her father's side full time. On the occasions when Martha Randolph could not be at the presidential home, Jefferson invited his secretary of state's wife, Dolley Madison, to assist him from time to time, and she delighted in her aggrandizement. With adroitness and the right amount of deference, both ladies were a success as the White House recovered from Jefferson's earlier exclusion of a feminine touch. Martha Randolph developed a formidable reputation as the nation's foremost hostess and displayed considerable courage and political acumen as she dealt with a delicate situation surrounding her father's personal life, helping him to evade the loss of his personal reputation and presidential prestige.

Neither Martha Randolph nor Dolley Madison altered the function of the First Lady role, though they did prevent the changes that might have occurred if Jefferson had carried out his original plan of working without an official hostess.

When James Madison was inaugurated as president in 1809, the already-experienced Dolley was in her element as the recognised nation's hostess. When she entered the White House as the president's wife, the house was still incomplete (Jefferson having shown little interest in improvements). Dolley was determined that improvements should begin immediately and with an appropriation of funds from Congress, she worked alongside the British architect Benjamin Latrobe to improve the house, which was completed in time for her first Drawing Room event. She planned the official state banquets, dinners, and receptions with her well-known aplomb and reinstated a full daily schedule of courtesy visits to wives and families of cabinet members, local dignitaries, and official visitors, all of which she considered essential to her role as First Lady. She nurtured her brilliant though shy husband through the social aspects of the presidency. A likeable man in private, Dolley realised that his innate shyness led to an unfortunate taciturn manner, and she would be at his side to charm everyone, avoiding the possibility of unwitting offence.

Always aware of the cabinet's agitation about Abigail Adams' perceived encroachment on political issues, Dolley avoided such circumstances. However, during the turmoil created by the 1812 war, President Madison was so unpopular that Dolley decided to intercede discreetly in the repercussions. Her covert manoeuvre proved her political acumen and was so skilfully executed, with a fortunate outcome, that it was not even noticed as an intervention. There is a question, however, as to whether this incident was a political interference, a practise eschewed by all factions since the Adams' era. Whatever answers modern readers may reach, it can be said that she fully and brilliantly maintained the pattern of social obligations within the First Lady role that her predecessors had established. While she did not improve or modify the role, the people of the era perceived her as a highly respected First Lady of the people.

Mrs. Madison's successor, Elizabeth Kortright Monroe, differed greatly. Even before James Monroe's inauguration in 1817, it was evident that the apparently aloof Mrs. Monroe would never allow others to determine her daily schedule. Elizabeth's reputation for unfriendliness had been formed during the previous eight years, when she had refused to socialise with other departmental wives during her husband's tenure as secretary of state. Although history has shown that Elizabeth was not without character and courage, she appeared at that time to lack the inclination and physical stamina to carry out the tasks of the nation's First Lady. During the first year of the Monroe administration, Elizabeth appeared infrequently at the White House official dinners and receptions. Consequently, wives and daughters of visiting congressmen and diplomats could not be invited to these events. Her long absences from Washington meant that the Drawing Room events were curtailed, and Elizabeth also refused to carry out any visiting schedules or even to return calls, though she was courteous enough to receive visitors. Her behaviour put increased strain on her relationships with diplomats and wives.

Eventually, congressmen, diplomats, and their wives became seriously offended at the social changes and vocalized their feelings to their cabinet colleagues. Supported by Louisa Adams, wife of the secretary of state, Elizabeth stuck firmly to her standpoint and gradually both she and Louisa were cold-shouldered when invitees to their receptions began to snub them. The situation reached an impasse when, on one occasion, only five women attended the First Lady's Drawing Room and only three turned up at one of Louisa Adams' departmental receptions.

Lengthy debate ensued, though no agreement was reached. The secretary of state, John Quincy Adams, wrote personal letters to the president and vice president outlining the reasons for the stance taken by the First Lady and his wife. He made it clear that neither had wavered from the concept of receiving invited guests and uninvited social visits with good grace. He also reiterated that their obligations to return social calls and to visit wives and families of incoming delegates, diplomats, and official guests were onerous and exhausting, leaving little private time available for their families. Soon after the secretary of state's intervention, the cabinet agreed that neither the First Lady nor the wives of cabinet members would be expected to act as a welcoming committee to every new legislator and family who moved to Washington unless they particularly wished to do so. This new policy became firmly established and was eventually accepted by everyone.

During Monroe's second term as president, Elizabeth's delicate health failed rapidly, and she was rarely seen in public, to the disappointment of the political and social elite. It would have been difficult for the Washington socialites and public to have visualised the woman of courage and fortitude she had once been when her husband had served as the U.S. minister to France, or that the people of Paris had adored and feted her. Whatever one might think of Elizabeth Monroe's tenure as America's First Lady, she did begin a process whereby the role entered a subtle new phase.

The next president, John Quincy Adams, may have intervened in Elizabeth Monroe's stance against the visiting schedules with an eye to his own future. As an astute politician, he would have recognised that a visit undertaken in bad grace could be detrimental, though they were also a way of establishing important social contacts. Therefore, when he was inaugurated as president in 1825, he informed his wife, Louisa, that some visiting by the First Lady may be necessary, while accepting that it would not become a matter of routine. He also assumed that his wife would be at home to receive all guests, invited or otherwise. Each time Congress convened, a new set of callers would arrive at their door, and it was anticipated that Louisa would receive a daily average of eight new visitors. John Quincy also had a habit of preparing a set of daily instructions for her, and more than once gave her only a short time to plan and prepare an important official dinner, sometimes for up to five hundred guests. With her usual efficiency, Louisa ensured that these were always successful. Much praise was heaped upon John Quincy's head, though he never passed this on to Louisa, who, usually exhausted with the daily routines and extra commitments, craved some acknowledgement of her efforts from her husband. It never came. Not once did the president appear to understand that the continuous heavy schedules placed upon his fragile wife could lead to exhaustion and consequent deterioration of her health.

Always the loyal wife, Louisa persevered with the daily commitments without complaint. She understood that politics was at the very core of her husband's life, though she never shared any part in that portion of his life. Neither did she attempt to spread her wings or raise her own profile during his presidency. She made little impact on the First Lady role other than her unswerving dedication to her husband and his career, against ever-increasing pressure. Her husband served only one term, and Louisa's profundity was never realised during his tenure. In later years, she was to become a catalyst for her husband's further political success and in setting the scene for future historians to chronicle an important era.

The image of these trailblazing women is one of extraordinary spirit, loyalty, and stamina. In many ways, they were innovators who collectively built the foundations of the role of First Lady, with modifications along the way, the most important being the stance taken by Elizabeth Monroe and Louisa Adams against visiting schedules. Little was known about the effects of physical and mental strain during that era, given the limited medical and psychological knowledge, and the stresses placed upon these women in their new role would not be tolerated in this modern age. Elizabeth Monroe may not have realised that some of her frailty, aloofness, and inability to cope could have been due to the prolonged fatigue and strain she experienced during her public service as James Monroe's wife, but she set an important precedent by taking herself away from the source during his second term. It is unfortunate that the physical condition of this misunderstood lady could not have been cited as a reason for her supposed antisocial behaviour without affecting her privacy. Had it been, she would surely have received understanding rather than reproaches, and future First Ladies may well have benefited from changes made as a consequence.

First Lady from 1789-1797

Martha Washington

(June 2, 1731 - May 22, 1802)

" I am determined to be cheerful and happy in whatever situation I may find myself. For I have learned that the greater part of misery or unhappiness is determined by our disposition"

Martha Washington

One Spring morning in 1789, a short, portly woman stepped ashore from a smart official-looking barge docked in Manhattan, New York, assisted by her dignified husband of thirty years. He was George Washington, the first president of the United States, a physically imposing man, standing well over six feet tall. The president was a highly prestigious man with a daunting task of ensuring a constitutional model of government for the new nation, a large concentration of land populated with around four million people. He had set a precedent that day as he arrived with his wife, a signal that she would play an important part in his new role. If Martha had wavered at the prospect, she was careful not to show it.

If one had said to Martha Dandridge, a timid girl born on a Virginia plantation fifty-eight years earlier, that she would be that woman, she might have run off to hide in shy fright. It was the same Martha, however, elegantly clothed in a flattering overdress of Indian silk and a white satin slip edged with Honiton lace. Even if she had wanted to hide away, Martha knew that she neither could nor would have done so.

This was her husband's destiny, and her loyalty toward him remained as intense as when they had first married.

Crowds lining the streets cheered the couple along the route from the harbour to the presidential home, a rented house on Cherry Street, just as they had done when a weary Martha had arrived in the city from Mount Vernon days earlier. Their cheers were not only for the president, but also for "Lady Washington," an affectionate title Washington's army had bestowed upon her during the War of Independence (1775–1783).

Martha Dandridge Washington was born in June 1731 on a New Kent plantation where she lived a privileged existence. She was the eldest child of John Dandridge who had emigrated from England in 1730, and Frances Jones of York County. Martha suffered tragedy early in her life, as four of her siblings died in infancy. This was a period of history when maternal and infant mortality was a common and predictable hazard in family life, the trauma of which affected Martha's psyche for the rest of her life.

Early records describe Martha as a child "gentle of manner." She was less than five feet tall and had dark hair and plain features, but those who knew her well looked beyond her lack of facial beauty, noticing only her vivaciousness and a ready, attractive smile.

The Dandridge family was not wealthy, but Martha grew up among prosperous, cultured plantation families, and she developed social skills, fashion sense, and impeccable manners. She had little formal education apart from basic math, reading, and writing and a heavy concentration on domestic arts. One of her chief hobbies was horse riding, and she became an excellent horsewoman. Although shy, she had a mischievous aspect to her nature. On one occasion, when visiting her Uncle William, it is alleged that she rode into his house, up the wide staircase, and down again. She was severely scolded by her family, except for her father, who laughed. "Let her alone," he said, "she has not harmed my brother's staircase, and by heavens, how she can ride."

Her family owned slaves, just like the majority of planters, and Martha accepted this as the way of life, an economic necessity in the running of the family farm. She always had a sense of fair play, however, and if she felt there was any injustice or mistreatment against the slaves on her father's farm, she would say so. Gossip of "forbidden" relationships between the races was often discussed, so it would not have surprised Martha when a strong rumour took hold that Ann Dandridge Costin, whose mother was of Cherokee and African origin, was her half sister, allegedly sired by her father, John Dandridge. Although this relationship has not been conclusively proven, Martha appeared to take a particular interest in Ann, and it is known that Ann lived within the Washington household for many years, eventually becoming the centre of a family scandal.

In spite of her limited education, Martha was a bright girl, and when she married Daniel Parke Custis, she developed management and farming skills in crop sales, animal husbandry, and homeopathic medicines, which came in handy as she progressed through her life. Martha's family

Bible recorded her wedding to Custis as May 1749, when she was eighteen and Daniel was thirty-eight. They had not had an easy courtship as Daniel's father, Colonel John Custis of Williamsburg, was opposed to Martha. He was socially snobbish and may have felt that his family, one of the richest in the county, was superior to hers. He had also disagreed with Martha's uncle during a local council meeting, resulting in the old chap detesting the whole Dandridge clan. John Custis had discussed the Dandridge family with close friends, describing Martha as a "gold digger." The couple kept their engagement secret while Daniel waited for the right time to discuss marriage with his father. Custis liked to keep his son under his thumb, and he often threatened to disinherit Daniel. Inevitably, word of the engagement got out and John Custis threatened to "throw away all his silver" before any of the Dandridge family "got their hands on it," stating that he would leave his plantation and wealth to the son of a Black slave. Custis had indulged a particular boy, Black Jack, since the boy had been born, and it was generally assumed that Custis was his father. Custis' high-ranking friends tried to reason with him for the sake of his only legitimate son, but he persisted with the threat.

Martha had never met her potential father-in-law and felt strongly that his bias was unjustified and unkind. A shy though determined seventeen-year-old, she declared she would visit Custis herself, and she did so, uninvited, taking him completely by surprise. Martha discussed her proposed marriage in a sweet-tempered way, and it seemed that her quiet, gentle manner, pleasing appearance, and decorum softened his attitude. He approved of her apparent strength of character, courteous manner, and lack of guile, realising that she was a striking girl anyone could welcome into their family. John deferred sanctioning the marriage, but after seeking further advice from his friends, he was eventually persuaded to accede. Before doing so, however, he exacted a promise from his son that, in the event of his death, Daniel would look after Black Jack until his seventeenth birthday, at which age the boy would inherit property that would establish him for life.

John Custis' last will, signed eight days before his death in November 1749, bequeathed his large estate to Daniel, who took Black Jack into the household. This unusual affiliation did not last long, however, as the child developed meningococcal meningitis at the age of twelve, from which he rapidly died in spite of intensive treatment and care.

Daniel and Martha Custis lived an opulent, happy life, and Martha bore four children, only two of whom survived, John (Jacky), born in 1754, and Martha (Patsy), born in 1756. The first two boys (Daniel and Frances) died in infancy, and it is said that the death of Frances hastened his father's demise. A grieving Martha was seriously traumatised when Daniel died suddenly and intestate at the age of forty-six in 1757. Alone with two small children, she set about managing the plantation and the administration of the estate's complex affairs, the skills for which had been honed throughout her marriage. The inheritance litigation was complicated, but the eventual settlement left Martha an extremely wealthy woman. She received her dower right of one-third of the net products of the

Custis lands, eighty-four slaves, a considerable cash sum, and the guardianship of her children, upon whom the balance of the 18,000-acre estate devolved. Martha's commercial competence was evident, especially in the handling of the plantation's tobacco crops, and she became a force to be reckoned with, as correspondence with London importers demonstrates.

Martha was a popular, winsome, and rich widow, and she had a number of suitors, though she showed no interest in any until she met George Washington at the home of a mutual friend in 1758. George was not aesthetically handsome, with his pockmarked face, substantial nose, decaying teeth, and huge hips, weighing in at around two-hundred pounds. However, his tall, upright figure conveyed a majestic, vigorous, magnetic presence whenever he entered any room. This charisma was his principal attraction, and when he was introduced to Martha, it was clear that she had fallen under the thrall of his aura. An immediate rapport was perceptible as he gazed down at her sweet, besotted face, and a betrothal soon followed. It is supposed that the young George was not unmindful of Martha's wealth, and many were to point out that others had already bewitched him in the recent past. His personal financial difficulties were also well known. Not surprisingly, these issues provoked gossip, which Martha wisely ignored.

The marriage took place at Martha's home, "The White House," on January 6, 1759. From the start, the marriage was one of mutual consideration and deep attachment as both looked forward to a peaceful life with Martha's children.

George was extremely fond of Jacky and Patsy and became their legal guardian by court order, and, in accordance with the property laws of that era, the ample Custis fortune came under Washington's trusteeship. This helped to advance him further into Virginia high society, much to his satisfaction.

When the couple first met, Washington was a colonel of the First Virginia Regiment. Martha may not have been willing to enter a marriage with the prospect of loneliness as the wife of a military officer, so it is not surprising that, shortly before the wedding, Washington resigned his commission. Eventually, it was decided that the family would live at the Washington estate Mount Vernon, which George had inherited upon the death of his brother, Lawrence. George and Martha spent the next sixteen years in a peaceful existence. George became an addict of horse racing, which took him far and wide. For his trips, he purchased an expensive, leather-lined carriage from London, bearing his own crest. He also took up card playing, usually breaking even, and he generally became the rural aristocrat he had always aspired to be. George spent much of his remaining time perfecting their beloved Mount Vernon home to his high standards. It could be said that the extensions, decorations, and furnishings were a showcase for the Washington ego, but the hospitable Martha felt at her happiest in that home.

Martha and George worked amicably as they engaged with their multiple family and plantation responsibilities together. They owned a large number of slaves between the two plantations, and their attitude to this ownership was typical of the general thinking of planters in that era—that the tradition of slavery was an economic necessity. Martha had grown up in that mode and accepted it fully, apparently giving no thought to the ethical and moral fundamentals. Still, she always remained compassionate about those in her care. Washington was also solicitous about the welfare of the slaves, and he warned his overseers not to overwork them and to inform him immediately if any disease broke out in the slave quarters. His main motive for this solicitation may have been to ensure a healthy, ongoing workforce at all times. If Martha was aware of his reasoning, she obviously accepted it because it meant the slaves remained well cared for.

Martha also approved of Washington's plan to build an elegant greenhouse in which they grew oranges. The couple would stroll through their elegant garden, often with guests. Many would comment on the elegance of the greenhouse, designed by Washington himself. They admired the way the buildings branched from the structure, providing an aesthetic balance, never realising that they were, in fact, cleverly disguised slave barracks.

Though there were occasional mild outbursts against the slavery system, the Civil War and slavery issues were so many years away that nobody considered the possibility of such a war or of slavery ending. However, George's experiences in the Revolutionary War eventually widened his outlook on the issue and he became more reproving of the institution. The idea of slavery began to repel him, especially after the birth of a son to Ann Dandridge, allegedly sired by Martha's son, Jacky. He believed that his stepson would have been as aware as everybody else of his likely kinship to Ann, and that both could and should have avoided a carnal relationship. The incident enraged and sickened him, for this was not the lust of a master for a slave; it was an incestuous relationship between a nephew and an aunt. A number of authors believe that this was one of the reasons why Washington stipulated in his final will that the Mount Vernon slaves should be freed upon his wife's death. He could not specify similar terms for the "dower" slaves who had formed part of Martha's inheritance from the Custis estate, as they, together with the Custis land, were entailed to Jacky or his heirs.

History has been denied intimate knowledge of the Washingtons' life together, as Martha destroyed all correspondence between them following his death. Yet, there is no doubt that the stewardship of the two estates provided a mutually peaceful, fulfilling existence. Martha took on the significant roles of directing the large staff and slaves of the two estates, ensuring fairness and compassion, while George oversaw financial transactions. He was also a committed member of the Virginia legislature.

Martha had always known George could be called out of private life should there be a military crisis, and in 1775, as war clouds rumbled, he was appointed commander in chief of the Continental Army. Although proud that her husband had been chosen to fulfil the essential role, Martha did not welcome the appointment, realising that their peaceful existence would disappear.

Throughout the war years, Martha spent summers at the

Mount Vernon and Custis estates to ensure the viability of their assets, but she followed her husband and his troops to the battlegrounds during the winters, enduring the same problems and deprivation the army suffered. Martha fully supported a formal endeavour to enlist women of the colonies to provide essential aid to troops, and she became a regular sight in the camps as she sat mending uniforms, talking to the troops, and ministering to the ill and injured soldiers. She encouraged army wives to mend and knit for the army, and also ensured that wives in other battle areas were apprised of the need to undertake similar work. Martha's cheerful presence heartened George and his troops, and the grateful men began to refer to her as "Lady Washington," a title which followed her for the rest of her life.

At the end of the war, Martha and George returned to Mount Vernon, where they enjoyed five years of tranquillity. Their peace was often disturbed by a steady stream of visitors eager to meet the great military hero, but Martha loved meeting these folks. Her natural warmth ensured social success, further enhancing Washington's reputation, and soon there was talk of nomination for president. Martha was disappointed at the prospect, having envisaged the rest of their life together peacefully managing their estates and enjoying their grandchildren. They had adopted Jacky's two younger children following his death from "camp fever" in 1781. Martha's daughter, Patsy, had died in 1773 from epilepsy.

As the clamour for George to stand as president grew, Martha bowed to the inevitable, and, with no other candidate, the people unanimously elected George, and he was inaugurated as the first president in 1789. As she joined her husband following his inauguration, "Lady Washington" impressed everyone with her dignified demeanour.

Martha willingly assumed management of their new home, though she did not relish the social demands abruptly placed upon her. Considerable discussions had already taken place concerning the role and work of the president's wife, but Martha had not been involved in any of the dialogue or decisions. It was agreed that the president would meet the role of government chief executive and also be called upon to meet as many people as possible, including congressmen, business leaders, and international grandees, as well as attend official functions as necessary. It was further mandated that the president would host a regular Tuesday afternoon "men only" formal event, known as a levee. In addition, he and his wife would be required to attend Thursday night state dinners for invited guests.

As the wife of the president, Martha was designated as hostess of a regular Friday evening reception known as a "Drawing Room," which the president would also attend. The regular event was intended as an informal "open house," and it was expected that those who attended would be "respectable" persons. Guests always enjoyed the Friday evening events, the president mingling with the callers while Martha herself remained seated to greet her guests, accompanied by Abigail Adams, wife of the vice president.

Martha did not take pleasure in her new role, especially the day following her arrival on Cherry Street, when she sat down with unknown guests who had been invited to "kick-start" the Friday Drawing Room. She was also expected to pay courtesy calls on families of local government officials as well as the families of visiting state governors and foreign leaders. Moreover, many of the social elite would call on Martha unbidden, and it was anticipated that she would return these unsolicited calls as a courtesy. She contrived to fulfil this particular duty within three days, enlisting help from Abigail Adams and other cabinet wives. There is little doubt that this sudden thrust into the limelight exhausted her as the heavy visiting schedules and social events became a prodigious burden.

Although onerous, the planned protocols, designed to ensure the president and his wife maintained a high profile, proved successful. According to Abigail Adams, Martha played a large part in their success. "Her manners are modest and unassuming, not the tincture of hauteur about her," she once told an enthralled audience. Mrs. Adams told another spellbound gathering about a recent visit to see the president's wife. She said, "A most becoming pleasantness sits upon her countenance and an unaffected deportment which renders her the object of veneration and respect. I found myself more deeply impressed than I ever did before their Majesties of Great Britain."

Eventually, the functions and government business increased to such an extent that the president's accommodation was moved to less confining, larger premises in Broadway, New York. Martha felt so delighted with this move that on Christmas Day 1789, she opened up her new home to local residents. A week later, many returned for her regular Friday Drawing Room which fell on January 1, 1790. George had postponed his Tuesday levee until that date to allow his and Martha's guests to join together to welcome the New Year. A tradition was born, and a similar event was held in the president's house on every New Year's Day (except in times of war and periods of mourning), for the next one hundred and forty-three years.

During the years, social events took place in ever-increasing numbers, and George reasoned that congressmen from every part of the United States should have access to him socially. A timetable was established for every congressman to visit annually, and Martha found herself even busier. A home-loving woman with a longing to return to normal life at Mount Vernon, Martha carried out the undertakings with uncomplaining fortitude, for the sake of her husband. She never allowed the public to recognise her oppression or to know that she felt her days as First Lady were "lost days." She once wrote to a niece that "I am more like a state prisoner than anything else. I live a very dull life here." She also complained to her friend, Mercy Warren, a respected historian, that she did not like "the ceremonies of mere etiquette that go with my unwished for situation."

The presidential home and offices moved again, this time to Philadelphia, where the social activities became more flamboyant. The large town house on High Street was enlarged further in order to accommodate a growing entourage, including a cream-coloured carriage and six horses. Gossips spoke of a presidency emulating a European royal court. Although Martha dressed tastefully, the dresses and jewels of the socialites became over-elaborate, and her receptions received press criticisms about their opulence and the "aloof and distant" manner of the president. Inevitably, public consternation about these social activities prompted many to accuse the president and his wife of being "too royal." During his second term, there were comments upon the president's policies and character based upon his so-called monarchical partialities. Martha endured these broadsides, realising that the comments emanated from her husband's political enemies and that she was powerless to stop them. In spite of this show of public discontent, however, her personal popularity remained as guests enjoyed her cordiality and courteousness.

Towards the conclusion of George's second presidential term, Martha and others began to notice that that the president's age was beginning to show as his eyesight and hearing deteriorated, and he occasionally allowed others to act on his behalf. Martha was glad when he declined an invitation to stand for a third term.

By this time, however, George Washington had clearly defined the two roles of the president of the United States as "Head of State" and "Head of Government." It was also established that the president's wife would not be involved in a government role, but instead, would play an essential part in state ceremonies as the nation's chief hostess and ambassadress. There is no evidence Martha ever had an indirect influence on George's administration, and most commentators believe that she did not. What is certain, however, is that she created a standard of behaviour for the First Lady that would last for many years.

George and Martha retired to Mount Vernon in 1797, where they resumed their former peaceful way of life. Martha wrote to a friend, stating she was "steady as a clock, busy as a bee and cheerful as a cricket." Their serene life together ended on December 14, 1799, when George died from surgery complications and a heart condition,

Martha remained well-off financially but handed over the practical control of her estates to her granddaughter, Eleanor (Nellie), and her husband, Lawrence Lewis. She retired to a comfortable, well-furnished suite of rooms within Mount Vernon and devoted herself to needlework, surrounded by her domestic slaves (often called house pets), including Ann Dandridge. Some have perceived Martha's attitude about keeping Ann Dandridge in slavery without attempting to free her as an act of philanthropy. The Virginia of the eighteenth century was not a place where a freed Black female slave could have achieved a good life, and perhaps the kindly Martha had felt that Ann would prosper more under her protection. Indeed, when Martha's personal maid, Oney Judge, fled from the Philadelphia household during the president's second term, she was devastated because she felt that the unsophisticated Oney, who later professed great regard for Martha, would be unable to care for herself. She was also saddened that her maid would want to leave her.

Following retirement, Martha rarely participated in social events. She ignored politics though she did have a rare lapse of diplomacy when she openly criticised the Jefferson administration. She did not like the new order of things inflicted by the widowed president, nor did she like the unproven gossip of a long-term relationship with a Black slave, who had allegedly bore him several children. It is not known whether Martha ever heard similar gossip regarding her husband's alleged relationship with the personal slave of his brother's wife, or the possibility that George had sired a son, West Ford, with her. If she had heard, she would probably have cast the rumours to one side in disbelief. This gossip has never been proved conclusively, in spite of painstaking research by modern scholars and the availability of current DNA science. Conclusive evidence cannot be provided as George Washington had no direct descendants from whom DNA samples could be taken.

Martha never recovered from the death of her husband, often saying, "I would like to join him now." She died from a severe fever in May 1802 at the age of seventy in the arms of her cherished granddaughter, Nellie, and lies buried at Mount Vernon beside George in the tomb enclosure which he had planned for them both as a final resting place.

First Lady from 1797-1801

Abigail Adams

(Nov 11, 1744 - Oct 28, 1818)

"I desire you would remember the ladies and be more generous and favourable to them than your ancestors."

Abigail Adams

Abigail Adams enjoyed presidential life with her husband, John Adams, the second president of the United States. During their fifty-four years marriage, she knew he regarded her as his intellectual equal and depended greatly on her counsel, as did her son, John Quincy Adams, who became the sixth president in 1825. She never doubted that women were as rational as men, and she made this clear in her habitually direct manner.

Abigail was born in November 1744. She was the second daughter of William Smith, a Congregationalist minister, and Elizabeth Quincy Smith. Her maternal grandfather, John Quincy, was a member of the Colonial Governor's Council and Speaker of the Massachusetts Assembly for 39 years from 1728. He greatly influenced Abigail and her three siblings.

The family lived in a sprawling parsonage overlooking their productive farm. As a quiet, stubborn girl with a tendency to minor illnesses, Abigail often complained of being smothered by her mother's fussing, though the balancing effect of their father's moderate style ensured the early years of the children were happy and secure. While her brother received a formal education, Abigail and her sisters were given only basic education as well as instruction in household management. However, their father had an excellent library to which the children were given full access, and Abigail, an avid reader, took full advantage of the facility. Her knowledge and mind developed from this daily exercise over the years, though her standards in spelling and writing remained poor throughout her life, a constant source of embarrassment. This self-education was a brave stance for a young woman of her times, one that enabled her to control her future destiny.

Abigail met John Adams at a family wedding in 1759, when she was fifteen and he was twenty-four. He later told a friend that she was "aloof," but when they met again two years later, John described her as "a modest, delicate, sensible, obliging, active girl, now grown up." Her love of reading also created a bond between the two, and Abigail was particularly fond of Shakespeare and Molière. She also loved music and taught herself French, all of which endeared her to the deep-thinking John. They were married on October 25, 1764, in her father's parsonage.

The couple began their extraordinary life in Braintree, Massachusetts (now Quincy). Abigail found herself preparing for motherhood almost immediately. Their first child was born in June 1765, just nine months after their wedding. Abigail gave birth to six children within the first eight years of marriage, two of whom died in infancy. They were: Abigail (Nabby), born 1765; John Quincy, born 1767; Charles, born 1770; Thomas, born 1772; Susannah, who died at the age of two years; and Elizabeth, stillborn in 1777.

John, the son of a New England farmer, was brought up in a setting of frugality and moderation, though his father ensured him a good education, and he became a Harvard-educated lawyer. He was never a rich man and with no inheritance to look forward to, he found it necessary to expand his law career in order to provide adequately for his family. The growth of his Boston law practice and career as a circuit judge entailed long absences from home, leaving Abigail to run their home and farm alone. However, she accepted the financial necessity for this unusual way of life and remained mindful of her husband's political aspirations, for which she was equally ambitious.

Early in his career, John Adams became identified with the patriot cause and was destined to become one of the leaders of the independence movement. He was a skilled orator and principled lawyer whose sense of justice gained him enemies when he once defended antislavery causes. This proved to be a trying time for Abigail, who feared on occasions for his personal safety. That, and his long absences, proved to be painful for both, but their solid love and regard for each other helped Abigail's loneliness, as did her children.

John and Abigail established intellectual companionship through letters. They shared political concepts as well as general household issues and local gossip. Abigail rarely grumbled, though she once proclaimed that she had been a "widow" for most of her married life. "Who shall give me back time?" she had wept. "Who shall compensate me for those years that I cannot recall?"

John's career progressed successfully, allowing them to move to Boston, where Abigail thrived on city life. There were homes of influential families to visit, and Abigail delighted in the accessibility of daily newspapers. It was during her cerebral conversations with new friends that she heard the first stirrings of revolution. John had been noticed for his ability to make a reasoned powerful case for America's disaffiliation from England, and it was no surprise that he was elected to the first Continental Congress in Philadelphia, which was formed in 1774. The Congress adopted a declaration of personal rights, denounced taxation without representation, petitioned the British Crown for redress, and called for the boycott of British goods. This meant longer absences from home because he was often in Philadelphia. Abigail disliked the situation, though she had no option but to accept it. John regretted the extra burden, including the education of his children which was placed upon his wife, but Abigail remained adamant that he must strive to achieve his highest ambition.

Their prolific correspondence continued, making it plain by the nature of their individual questions and advice to each other that their relationship was a merging of minds. Abigail also found solace in writing to associates and long-standing friends, including Thomas Jefferson and John Lovell (a prominent Continental Congress delegate). Education for women was a strong theme in many of Abigail's letters to her husband, and she often bemoaned her own lack of formal education. Her logic matched that of her friend, socialite and historian Mercy Warren, who felt that since women were responsible for the early education of children, they themselves should be well educated.

When the first shots of the American Revolutionary War were fired in 1775, the Massachusetts General Court was concerned by the number of women who had been charged with either remaining loyal to the British Crown or working against the Independence Movement. Consequently, the court established a panel of intellectual women to be responsible for interviewing these apparent traitors. Abigail was appointed to the panel, along with Mercy Warren and Hannah Winthrop (the governor's wife). Abigail and John were honoured that she had been recognised as worthy of the role.

With her sharp mind already honed by conversations with her educated friends, Abigail discussed American Libertarian objectives with John, stating that they fell short of the original intention. She referred particularly to slavery, which she was very much against, and told John in a number of letters to him that she wished there was not one slave in the province.

John Adams, Thomas Jefferson, and James Madison worked hard on the draft of the Declaration of Independence, which was debated by the Continental Congress, and during this time, Abigail wrote one of her best-known appeals to her husband. "I desire you to remember the ladies and be more generous and favourable to them than your ancestors. Do not put unlimited power into the hands of husbands." John was impressed with her thoughts but did not take her petition seriously, calling it "saucy." "We know better than to repeal our masculine system," he replied, "and though they are in full force, you know they are little more than theory. We are obliged to go fairly and softly." Abigail would not be put off by his approach. She wrote back, "I cannot see that you are very generous to the ladies, for whilst you are proclaiming peace and good-will to men, emancipating all nations, you insist upon retaining absolute power over wives." The letter castigated all men, but did not achieve any changes.

Abigail was not, however, as militant as her letters might suggest. Neither did she make public demands for the rights of women, though she made it clear that there should be more equality for education and legal affairs. Her overtly expressed strong views and her sharp tongue were criticised extensively by the press and a spiteful male faction in Boston, but somehow, her sunny nature prevailed.

John also served in the Second Continental Congress and in 1778 was appointed as U.S. commissioner to France. Abigail travelled with him to Paris, where they remained for eighteen months, often meeting up with John's good friend, Thomas Jefferson, whom Abigail liked and respected, as well as Benjamin Franklin. In 1785, John was appointed as the first U.S. ambassador to Great Britain. Abigail travelled on the SS Active to join her husband at his post, and was the first American woman to be presented at the Court of St. James. Abigail disliked the court who, following the recent political history between the two countries, reacted with disdain towards the American ambassador and his wife. Abigail reciprocated coldly, though with dignity and tact, and John ensured that his demeanour was impeccable, intent on completing his diplomatic duties with honour. Although they made few friends within the royal circle, Abigail enjoyed the pomp and circumstance of the European royal courts, though she never forgave the British for the discourtesy shown to her husband and his role. They returned in 1788 to a handsome house in Braintree (later renamed Quincy), which was to be their family home for the rest of their lives.

When John Adams was appointed as vice president to George Washington in 1789, Martha Washington sought the assistance of his wife in the heavy hostess role. Abigail's experience within the European courts proved an asset, and the two women became friends. Abigail spent as much time as she could in support of Mrs. Washington, though she was obliged to travel to Braintree at frequent intervals, realising that continued management and maintenance of their assets remained a priority in view of the family's limited financial resources.

When John succeeded as president in 1797, the illness of her mother-in-law prevented Abigail from attending the inauguration ceremony, though she joined her husband in Philadelphia soon afterwards, in response to his written plea. In a letter imploring her to join him, he said, "I never wanted your advice and assistance more in my life." She found that the role of wife to the president was preferable to that of the vice president, but regretted that her receptions, which were more formal than those of Martha Washington, could not be as sumptuous as she would have liked, and that she was unable to spend as much time in Philadelphia as she wished. Their financial position was a constant worry to Abigail, and the additional financial burdens of office meant careful expenditure and frequent scrutiny and management of their personal assets.

When she was in Philadelphia, however, Abigail made a strong impression on the press and public. She performed her role within the established protocol and became known for her witty conversation and vivacity, though she tended to receive visitors more formally than her predecessor, perhaps influenced by her European visits. Abigail also attempted to influence fashion. She believed the current trends were unbecoming, but her limited funds required cautious personal spending, and her attempts fell flat.

Archived correspondence discloses that John discussed many important problems with his wife during his presidency, even engaging her assistance in drafting semi-official letters. Critics began to notice that those who sought the approval of the president would often present themselves to Abigail first, though she always denied this. Her growing reputation as the presidential "right hand" resulted in criticism in the press and in Congress. In her usual way, Abigail overcame the criticism and remained resolute that she would be of assistance to her husband whenever she could. She continued to advise him, and he continued to seek her support.

They disagreed on only one major issue, which concerned

the relations between the United States and France over the French seizure of American merchant ships. A breaking point was reached in 1798, when the Federalists favoured war, as did Abigail. The president appeared to be leaning heavily towards war, and was even preparing for it, but to the surprise of everyone, including Abigail who was not in Philadelphia at the time, Adams appointed Elbridge Gerry to head a peace mission to France. Abigail was even more surprised when friends informed her that some of her critics had said they wished "the old woman had been there" to stop the president's action. John wrote to her himself, saying that Federalists had been outraged at his decision. "How they lament Mrs. Adams' absence," his letter said. Far from being gratified, Abigail deplored the fact that her dissension from John's views had been made public, and when the peace mission proved successful, Abigail publicly acknowledged her husband's wisdom, stating that this was his greatest achievement.

Meanwhile, the strong friendship between the president and Thomas Jefferson suffered. The estrangement was heightened when John signed the Alien and Sedition Acts, which Jefferson strongly opposed. This opposition, as well as the French affair, contributed to Jefferson's decision to stand against his former friend in the 1800 presidential election.

Immediately prior to the November election that John Adams was expected to win, the federal administration moved from Philadelphia to the unfinished government building in Washington. It took the family a whole week to journey there and en route, they lost their way in Baltimore and many of their own family heirlooms were lost, broken, or stolen, which upset the family greatly. They arrived on October 16, 1800, to find the large living quarters cold and damp, with only six rooms completed. There were no staircases and no personal conveniences. Abigail ordered fires to be lit and maintained constantly in order to dry out the rooms and make them habitable. In the largest room, which had two fireplaces, now known as the East Room, she was obliged to set up a laundry with drying lines spanning the area. The site surrounding the building was muddy, with dust abounding everywhere. Abigail's usual cheerful nature triumphed once again, and she refused to feel the slightest bit sorry for herself as she coped in those difficult early days in the presidential mansion. With hard work and the goodwill of her staff, the White House gradually thawed out and was cleaned and furnished quite respectably by the end of the year so that the presidential couple were able to hold their first reception on New Year's Day, 1801. This was a huge success, and hundreds turned out to see the president's new home.

John and Abigail were shocked when their former friend, Thomas Jefferson, ousted them in a bitter, tightly run race. Their unhappiness at losing the election was intensified by the sudden death of their second son, Charles, whose wanton life had been a source of great concern for many years. The couple returned unenthusiastically to their home in Quincy, but, true to her nature, Abigail recovered from the devastating blows and eventually helped John accept the different way of life. She wrote to her daughter, telling her of how she could often be found skimming milk at five o'clock in the morning and of how her father liked to spend his July mornings in the fields attending his haymakers.

There were no more separations. Abigail enjoyed being a full-time housewife, mother, and grandmother, and she watched John Quincy's progress in his political career with the same pride she had when he was a child. John and Abigail abandoned the Federalists, having supported the Republican candidate, James Madison, at the end of Jefferson's presidency in 1809, though their lives were not now filled with political issues.

This was a welcome change for Abigail, though her life was severely blighted when her beloved daughter, Abigail (Nabby), died of breast cancer. Nabby's husband, William Smith, a distant cousin, had left his family years earlier in order to fulfil his career dreams, so it was left to Abigail and John to bring up her children, which they did willingly. Their son, Charles, had married Smith's sister, and on his death, John and Abigail asked their daughter-in-law and her children to live with them, which suited Abigail very well, surrounded as she was by their grandchildren. At last she was able to live the life she had dreamed of for so long. They were a happy couple, and the press dubbed them "Darby and Joan."

The last years of Abigail's life were not good, as she was frequently ill and often confined to her bed for days, and sometimes weeks, at a time. She suffered a number of illnesses, one of them being St. Anthony's Fire, a severe skin inflammation, now known as erysipelas, which caused her great discomfort. Often sick and depressed, her natural, cheerful temperament and religious faith ensured that she did not remain despondent for long. Weakened by illness, she succumbed to typhus fever in 1818, which affected her liver, and died a few days before her seventy-fourth birthday.

John was, of course, devastated. He told their son, John Quincy, that she had been his never-failing support and that he felt he could not make it without her at his side. He did make it, however, for another eight years and happily saw their son, John Quincy, become the sixth president. He continued to miss Abigail, and during one of his most despondent days, he decided to write to his former friend, Thomas Jefferson, to inform him of his dear wife's death. In his letter, he stated that he felt Jefferson, who had also suffered from the death of his own wife so many years earlier, would understand his current state of mind. Both Adams and Jefferson welcomed their reconciliation which began a long and lengthy correspondence that illuminated their opposed political philosophies. Thomas Jefferson died a few hours prior to his old friend John Adams, on July 4, 1826, exactly fifty years after the signing of the Declaration of Independence, though John did not know this. As he closed his eyes for the last time, John Adams spoke his final words, "Jefferson survives."

Abigail would have agreed with Edward Everett, a statesman and orator, who delivered a eulogy to Adams and Jefferson in commemoration of the two friends on August 1, 1826, in Charlestown, Massachusetts. He said, "Such men do not, cannot die; this is not the end of existence to the men who breathed their spirits into the institutions of their country, who have stamped their characters on the pillars of age, who have poured their hearts' blood into the channels of public prosperity."

Abigail was never close to John Quincy's wife, Louisa, though it was Louisa who chronicled many of Abigail's letters, leaving historians with remarkable facts of those times. She also inspired John Quincy to carry on his mother's early battles on education and rights for women, and he achieved some success. Louisa's sentiments about the legacy left by Abigail would probably be similar to those of Edward Everett, and there can be no doubt that John Adams would have asked that Everett's words be dedicated to Abigail, his wife, his steady rock, his soul mate.

Martha Jefferson

October 19, 1748 - September 6, 1782

Martha Jefferson died 18 years before Thomas Jefferson was inaugurated as President in 1801. Their daughter, Polly Jefferson Randolph, served as the White House hostess on occasion. Both women are included in the biographical list of first ladies

The Jefferson Ladies

Martha Wayles Skelton Jefferson
(wife of Thomas Jefferson)

Martha "Patsy" Jefferson Randolph
(daughter of Thomas Jefferson)

Thomas Jefferson had been a widower for nineteen years when he became the third United States president in 1801. He had married Martha (Wayles) Skelton, daughter of barrister John Wayles and Martha (Eppes) Wayles, and widow of attorney Bathurst Skelton, on New Year's Day in 1772. Born on October 19, 1748, Martha was an attractive and cheerful individual, well educated for her day, and a constant reader. A shared love of music had brought the couple together.

Martha had always played a part in politics as her husband's career prospered. George Washington's wife had recognized Mrs. Jefferson's efficiency and asked her to "lead a list of prominent Virginia women in donating necessities and financial support, and other voluntary efforts, on behalf of the Continental Army." She led the successful mission, earning the gratitude of many, including the president's wife. There is no doubt that had she lived to become the First Lady, Martha would have fulfilled the role with self-assurance, style, and compassion.

The couple moved to the Jefferson home, Monticello, in

Charlottesville, Virginia, following their wedding, and during their ten years of marriage, Martha gave birth to five children. Only two of the children survived infancy: Martha ("Patsy"), born in 1772, and Maria ("Polly"), born in 1778. A daughter, Jane, born in 1774, had survived for only twelve months; a son, born in 1777, lived only a few days; Lucy, the youngest, died in 1785 at three years old.

Subdued and worn out, Martha never regained her strength following her final pregnancy in 1782, and she died in September of that year. Thomas hardly left his wife's side during her last brief illness, and he missed sessions of the Virginia General Assembly and refused a post abroad in order to be with her. On her death, Thomas was so overcome with grief that he fainted and remained unconscious for so long that it was feared he would not recover. His personal sorrow was overwhelming and his ten-year-old elder daughter, Patsy, arranged for someone to be at his side every moment. Eventually, he recovered enough to take walks with Patsy by his side, who once wrote that she witnessed many violent outbursts of grief. He burnt all the correspondence between them shortly after his wife's death and seldom spoke of her.

Patsy remained a source of comfort to her father after her mother's untimely death. She was herself heartbroken and became even more so at witnessing the decline of her beloved father during the following years as she encouraged him back to his personal and political life. Eventually, he was able to return to politics and took an interest in education, though this did not extend to his daughters.

When he was appointed as minister to France in 1785, Jefferson took his surviving daughters, Patsy and Polly, with him. The family was accompanied by a slave girl, Sally Hemings, who acted as maid and chaperone to the girls. Jefferson enrolled his daughters into the Abbaye Royale de Panthemont, an exclusive convent school, with assurances that they would, as Protestants, be excluded from religious instruction. He quickly withdrew them, however, when Patsy began to talk about becoming a nun. They received a basic education from a private tutor from then on. He tended to lecture his daughters, and on the day of Patsy's wedding to Thomas Mann Randolph in 1790, Jefferson told her that "The happiness of your life depends now on continuing to please a single person. To this, all other objects must be secondary." He also advised his daughters to avoid novels and poetry and instead focus on drawing, music, French, and needlework, and emphasised that the efficient running of a household was essential. Patsy always remembered his homilies, but would continue to regret the lack of a more formal education.

Jefferson's mother-in-law had unwittingly set the course by which he would ultimately become notorious. On her marriage to John Wayles, she had inherited an African slave with an infant daughter as part of her dowry. The infant of mixed race, the result of a liaison with an English sea captain named Hemings, was called Betty, who became a concubine of John Wayles many years later. She bore him six children, half siblings to his legitimate children. A number of these children, among them Sally Hemings, had been endowed to Martha (Wayles) Skelton as part of her dowry, and they followed their mistress to Monticello following her wedding to Thomas Jefferson. Jefferson tended to keep the Hemings family close to him as his personal servants, and they served him loyally for many years. Sally, however, would eventually be the cause of much humiliation and gossip.

Sally Hemings was a good-looking girl with pale coffee-coloured skin and long, black, straight hair, which belied her heritage at first glance. Jefferson was surprised to find that Sally wished to remain in Paris to live as a free woman when his term as minister to France was completed, but he bargained with her and promised that upon his death, she would be freed. She returned to Monticello on that promise.

There had been gossip about Jefferson's alleged relationship with Sally in France, with constant strong rumours on his return to America that he favoured one of his slaves and that she had borne him several children. His opponents were quick to seize on the scandal when he was nominated for president, and the rumours quickly spread as his opponents used the gossip to undermine him. Supporters of John Adams, the incumbent president hoping to win a second term, may have begun the gossip during the "dirty" campaign. Adams and Jefferson had spent much time together in France and had been firm friends until Jefferson decided to stand against him, which gave a measure of credence to the accusations of Adams' campaigners.

In spite of the tittle-tattle and damaging rumours, Jefferson won the close-fought election by a narrow margin, becoming the third president of the U.S. in 1801, serving for two terms.

It was clear from the beginning that this would be a different presidency in terms of the White House social calendar. The role of the First Lady had become more or less established over the previous twelve years and Washingtonians watched to see how a widowed president would manage. Jefferson began his tenure in the way he had planned, with no pomp, procession, or special dress as he marched unceremoniously, and alone, across the road for his inauguration, his long boots providing protection against the mud and puddles of the unfinished paths. No family members were present.

Jefferson's vice president, Andrew Burr, was also a widower. Therefore, he could not offer the services of his wife to assist in the First Lady role. However, Jefferson believed that the role of official hostess was not necessary (except as an escort at some official gatherings), and he considered that the social and political receptions and dinners should be reduced or cancelled where possible. He also felt strongly that the White House public engagements that were held could and should be managed by the White House staff. As a connoisseur of good food and wine, he was willing to share his expertise with appropriate staff through his personal chef and valet (both members of the Hemings clan), who supervised the events. He shunned ceremony and declared a "free and easy" policy of seating. He would sit at official dinners where his fancy took him and encouraged others to do the same. He gave the impression that he would personally fulfil the role of national host, much to the dismay of many.

It did not take long, however, before Jefferson realised that an official hostess was necessary, and he sought the help of his daughter, Patsy Randolph. She had plenty on her plate already with her six children. She would produce a further six within the next fifteen years. In spite of her heavy personal load, Patsy quickly established herself as the nation's hostess, and is now officially listed as America's third First Lady. She was not always available due to her family commitments. On those occasions, either her younger sister, Maria, or the wife of Jefferson's secretary of state, Dolley Madison, assisted Patsy. The three women brought a breath of fresh air, youth, and vivacity to what was becoming a socially dull presidency.

Patsy was tall and slender, with shiny red hair and angular features similar to those of her father. She became a popular figure around the White House and proved to be an efficient household manager and a charming hostess but was unable to spend much time at her father's official home. The longest periods she was in residence at the White House were during the winters of 1802 and 1806. She bore four of her children during the presidency, one of whom, James Madison Randolph, born on January 17, 1806, was the first ever child to be born in the White House.

Patsy occasionally found her lack of formal education to be a handicap. Even without it, she had earned a reputation for intellectual abilities and political guile. During Jefferson's first term as president, the gossip about his alleged relationship with Sally Hemings had escalated and Patsy was aware that the rumours could ultimately damage his personal reputation and presidency. She persuaded her father to attend the Sunday religious services held in the Hall of Congress, ensuring that he was always accompanied by one of his daughters and grandchildren. The public noted and welcomed the family parade at church and many either forgave him his alleged indiscretions or decided not to believe the gossip. Patsy astutely elected to spend the winter of 1802 at the White House with her family during the height of the scandal.

Patsy undertook the task of managing the Monticello estate during Jefferson's presidency. She had constant contact with Sally Hemings and her children there and found herself in the position of supervising her half aunt and her father's alleged mistress as a privileged house servant. She felt, however, she neither could nor would ever acknowledge their blood ties or those of Sally's offspring. It would be over two hundred years before the rumours could be confirmed as true by meticulous research and modern scientific tests.

Jefferson had an overall satisfactory presidency. He reduced the national debt by a third, acquired the Louisiana Territory from Napoleon, and kept the nation from involvement in the Napoleonic wars. Upon completion of his presidency in 1809, Patsy returned full time to her own home, Edgehill, where she lived with her family. Following her father's death on July 4, 1826 (the same day as John Adams), Patsy discovered that he had incurred considerable debts at Monticello, which had been left to her (her sister having died in childbirth). Her own financial position had been severely jeopardised due to the mental illness of her now-estranged husband who died shortly afterwards, and Patsy had no other option but to sell Monticello and Edgehill in order to repay the debts. After losing her home and financial status, she lived with her daughter, Ellen Coolidge, and her husband for a time. She eventually moved in with her younger daughter, Septima, and her husband in Washington. She was happier there, and she became a popular and favourite figure amongst the Washington socialites and remained a frequent guest of President Andrew Jackson at the White House. Unfortunately, a plea from congressmen loyal to Thomas Jefferson for a pension "in respect for her father and the role she had played in his presidency" as the nation's third First Lady was not granted. Patsy Jefferson Randolph died in October 1836. She lies buried next to her husband and father in Monticello.

First Lady from 1809-1817

$\mathscr{Dolley\,Madison}$

May 20, 1768 - July 12,1849

*"There is one secret, and that is the the power we all have in forming
our own destinies."*

Dolley Madison

James Madison, the fourth U.S. president, was proud of his wife, a senior member of Washington society who is remembered with deep affection. She was a woman adored for her vitality, charm, and generosity, and many socialites in the early nineteenth century attempted to emulate her. The Washingtonians named her "Queen Dolley" because she added a new dimension to the White House following the Jefferson era. Mary Bayard Smith, a chronicler of early Washington social life, once wrote, "She looked like a Queen. It would be absolutely impossible for anyone to behave with more propriety than she did."

Born into a Quaker family, her birth in Piedmont, North Carolina, on May 20, 1768, had been recorded in the New Garden monthly meeting of the Society of Friends as "Dolley, daughter of John and Mary Cole Payne, settlers from Virginia." Her grandfather, John Payne, an English gentleman, had migrated to Virginia, but Dolley and her seven siblings did not enjoy a life of rank or wealth. Neither did they acquire the skills of music, dance, painting, or household management. Indeed, these accomplishments were anathema to the Society of Friends, of which her austere parents were members, though the girls were taught elementary reading, writing, and math by their brothers' tutor.

Dolley's family returned to Virginia when she was a small child, and she grew up with her siblings on their father's plantation within a Quaker community. She found it difficult to conform to the strictness of her community's authority, and nothing quelled her happy and warm personality. Putting decorum to one side, she would often hitch up her skirts into her underwear and run races with her brothers, risking the displeasure of her father. What she would have done without her maternal grandmother, who saved her skin on a number of occasions, is anybody's guess. Dolley learned from her grandmother to be creative in cooking and dressmaking, and she gained an interest in quality food, fashion, fabric, and fine art. She always maintained that her grandmother was the most influential person in her life.

In 1783, her father freed his slaves and moved his family to Philadelphia, a leading commercial and cultural centre, where he established himself as a starch merchant. During the 1780s, Philadelphia was beleaguered by economic turbulence, and by the end of the decade, Payne's business had collapsed, resulting in financial upheaval for the family. The Society of Friends disowned him for the sin of becoming insolvent, and with no other alternative, her mother turned their home into a boarding house, where Dolley became the cook.

During that time she met John Todd, a Quaker lawyer, whom she married in 1790 at the age of twenty-one, and bore two sons (John Payne Todd in 1792 and William Isaac in 1793). Dolley's father died in 1792, and a year later, the Yellow Fever plague struck Philadelphia. Accounts of the epidemic confirm the harrowing deaths of complete families, the orphaning of children, and the unsanitary conditions of streets and homes. Not fully understanding the nature of the disease, physicians could not cope. John Todd moved his wife and sons to a countryside resort outside of the city, but it turned out that the disease had already reached that area. Their younger son, William, succumbed to the fever on October 14, 1793, and John died shortly afterwards, on the same day. John's parents followed quickly, leaving Dolley a widow at twenty-five, with neither a father nor a father-in-law who could guide her. Fortunately, she had sufficient funds to care for her remaining son, John, but was uncertain how long she could remain solvent.

By that time, Philadelphia had become the capital city and George Washington had been elected to a second term as president. Dolley's sister, Mary, had married Washington's nephew and introduced Dolley into society. With her good looks, gregarious personality, and renowned charm, it was not long before Dolley was attracting considerable attention. New York senator Aaron Burr, destined to be Jefferson's vice president, and who lived in her mother's boarding house, was an admirer. Dolley rejected his advances as she did those of other suitors, but in May 1794, she wrote to her best friend, Elizabeth Collins, that "... the great little

Madison has asked to see me this evening." She agreed to meet him that evening and many others thereafter. James Madison was an Episcopalian, seventeen years her senior, and shorter in stature, all of which created doubt in her mind at the beginning of the courtship. However, as their relationship grew, none of those factors mattered, and they married in September 1794.

James Madison had a reputation as a quiet, erudite thinker who had played an important part in the writing of the American Constitution. The Constitutional Convention, made up of fifty-five members, gathered daily to revise the Articles of Confederation, though it soon became apparent it would not be sufficient to simply amend the Articles. A new document was required to define the powers of central government and of individual states, people's rights, and how representatives should be elected. This was completed in September 1787, and copies of the Constitution were sent to the state legislatures for ratification. Madison, Alexander Hamilton, and John Jay wrote the Federalist Papers in support of the final document. By June 21, 1788, nine states had approved the Constitution, and the Union was formed. During the Constitutional debates, Madison took copious and meticulous notes of the procedure, and these notes eventually became important national documents of historical importance.

Notably happy from the start, James and Dolley's marriage was childless, though James enjoyed fathering his stepson, John, who would, in later years, prove to be a problem to them. Disowned by the Quakers for marrying outside her faith, Dolley discarded her sombre Quaker dress and chose the finest fashions, colourful fabrics, and elegant shoes. Her charisma and dress sense, both nurtured as a child by her grandmother, made her a favourite among the Philadelphia elite. Gradually, Dolley became the country's leader of fashion, and she delighted in trying out new styles of gowns, shoes, hats, and hair. She was the first to reveal cleavage and wear dresses with trains in the name of fashion, and on one memorable occasion, she used a parrot as an accessory.

She blossomed socially, both in Philadelphia and at her husband's Virginia home, Montpelier, where she presided over dinner parties and attended balls. Her dancing skills quickly developed, and at a 1795 presidential ball, President Washington remarked that Mrs. Madison was the sprightliest partner he had danced with. Members of society prized an invitation to her home, and no one who attended her receptions would ever have suspected her strict upbringing. She eventually became an Episcopalian.

In 1801, James was appointed as President Jefferson's secretary of state. Dolley, who wished so much to please the man who made her so happy, moved willingly with him to Washington. In addition to her natural charm, Dolley cultivated the graciousness required of her position as James' wife, and invitations to their successful diplomatic dinners were eagerly accepted. Always fond of good food, Dolley decided to feature typical American dinners, and she sought traditional recipes from far and wide. It was not long before people in Washington and beyond were clamouring to obtain her recipes.

In her capacity as wife of the secretary of state, Dolley often acted as official hostess for President Jefferson, particularly when his daughter, Martha Randolph, was unable to preside at events that required a hostess to receive the female guests. Dolley was happy to do this for the sake of her husband, and she carried out the duties with such finesse that her fame spread.

James Madison knew that one of his wife's assets (which he never publicly recognised) was her political acumen. He saw that her warmth, graciousness, and sense of tact dissolved many a quarrel, and this left hostile statesmen, difficult European envoys, and even warrior chiefs in her thrall. She failed only once, during a particularly difficult relationship with a British envoy. The envoy's wife had officially complained that the secretary of state had ignored her at a reception, and the relationship with the British embassy deteriorated. Eager to close a widening breach, Dolley made several unsuccessful attempts at reconciliation. She agreed to try one more time, and she arranged a special informal dinner to honour the British envoy. All went well at the reception, and James escorted the envoy's wife to the dinner table. During dinner, she apparently realised that she was seated next to a haberdasher and his wife who had been invited for their witty conversation. This was taken as a deliberate insult to her and after dinner, she was overheard to say that the evening had been more like a harvest supper than the entertainment of the secretary of state. Dolley replied courteously, stating that she did not "hesitate to sacrifice the delicacy of European taste for the less elegant but more liberal fashion of Virginia." That particular envoy was never again invited to attend a Madison social reception.

In 1809, James Madison was inaugurated as the fourth President of the United States and the experienced Dolley became First Lady. The term "First Lady" had not yet entered the American vocabulary so she was affectionately known as "the Presidentress." It is widely supposed, however, that she was referred to as America's First Lady at her funeral, though there is no record of the existence of that eulogy. Dolley, who had often thought the White House was in need of loving care, was able to invite a number of senators and congressmen to see what was required. It was not long before Congress appropriated funds for renovation, and Dolley employed a prominent architect, Benjamin Latrobe, with whom she worked closely.

Within a few months, the work was completed and Dolley recommenced receptions and dinners, hired the best chefs and a master of ceremonies, and expanded her guest lists to include writers and artists. These events, as well as her regular Friday Drawing Rooms, became a popular topic in Washington. Unlike those of the Adams and Jefferson years, the entertainments were lavish, and with her friendly, kind, unassuming effervescence, Dolley became renowned as the most famous and popular hostess in America. She clearly loved her role as she generously entertained visitors, returned calls, and initiated visits to the wives of diplomats and envoys. Recipients looked forward to her invitations and calls with enthusiasm.

Aware of the criticisms surrounding Abigail Adams, Dolley always took care never to take an active part in state affairs, and she showed no favouritism among her husband's acquaintances, whether they were for him or against him. During the 1812 War, known as Mr. Madison's War (when he declared war on the British, believing that they were intent on the permanent suppression of American commerce), Dolley did not become overtly involved in the resulting turmoil, but she watched with concern as the opposition Federalists planned the shipping of their goods via Canada. As protestors from the president's own party began to decline invitations to dine at the White House, or even speak with the president, Dolley's discreet interference proved that she had considerable political acumen and resourcefulness. With her usual cheerful demeanour, she resolved to do something about the situation. She established a series of personal visits to all of the congressmen's families who had moved to Washington. By initiating the house calls, Dolley signalled humility, and when each of the families later received, and accepted, an invitation to the White House, she was delighted, even though it had placed an extra burden upon her.

Not long afterwards, she became a public heroine. On August 24, 1814, James was away from Washington, on the front lines with his troops, and he ordered his wife to leave at once for Virginia. She refused to do so, preferring to be "at home" when James returned. She stayed within the White House until around 1:30 p.m., when she heard cannon fire. Having already commandeered a large wagon, she and her staff moved quickly, loading it with vital government documents, presidential papers and books, and the most valuable silver and china. The most important item saved was the famous painting of George Washington by the artist Gilbert Stuart. Realising that the frame was too heavy for easy handling, she asked servants to climb on chairs to cut the picture from the frame. She then drove off with the loaded wagon and her good friend, Matilda Love, who had hastened to the White House to persuade Dolley to leave. They made their way to the home of Virginian friends. Shortly after their departure, the British army invaded Washington and set fire to the White House and other government buildings.

When James arrived back at the White House three days later, he was surprised to find that Dolley had returned. Upon her arrival in the city, she had been greeted by cheering crowds. "We shall rebuild Washington City, the enemy cannot frighten a free people!" she called to them. Undaunted, though their home was in ruins, Dolley immediately launched a campaign for rebuilding the White House and the city. She continued to entertain, and she impressed everyone with her spirit, which had the effect of stabilising the nation as well as the city.

James Madison served two terms as president, and was succeeded by James Monroe in 1817. He and Dolley returned to Montpelier, where as mistress of the estate, she continued to entertain on a large scale. They received many visitors, one of the most notable being the Marquis de Lafayette. Following his visit, the Marquis remarked, "Nowhere have I encountered a lady who is lovelier or more steadfast."

She constantly supported her husband, who continued his public spirited work. He worked closely with Thomas Jefferson in creating the University of Virginia, serving as rector from 1826 to 1836. Eventually, her husband's health declined. Old and frail as he was, however, James retained his sharp mind, and continued to comment on politics and wrote or dictated numerous letters and notes until the time of his death. Dolley spent many hours reading to him or taking dictation as he voiced his erudite thoughts. Shortly before his death in 1836, he dictated a message to the nation, "Advice to my Country," which he sealed and ordered that it should not be opened until after his death. The message, in Dolley's handwriting, began, "The advice nearest to my heart is that the Union of the States be cherished and perpetuated."

During this period, they were concerned by the antics of Dolley's wayward son. He was often in debt and had been thrown into a debtor's prison on at least two occasions. When her husband died, Dolley found that she had to sell the family home and most of John's property to settle her son's debts. Following this trauma, she returned to Washington, a popular figure still. She received hundreds of calling cards and invitations from public figures such as Daniel Webster, Winfield Scott, John Quincy Adams, and President Van Buren.

Knowing she was hard-pressed financially, Congress appropriated money to purchase her husband's papers, which included the historic notes he had taken at the Constitutional Convention of 1787. This sale eased her modest financial resources. Even so, she was forced to limit her entertaining to one reception per month. Invitations to this event were always eagerly awaited and accepted with fervour, for she had lost none of her flamboyant confidence. Following one of her events, President Van Buren exclaimed that Mrs. Madison was the most brilliant hostess the country has ever known, and Daniel Webster told her that she was the only permanent power in Washington.

Stories still abound about Dolley Madison and the influence she had on presidencies and the Capitol over her last years. When she died in 1849 at the age of eighty-one, she was greatly mourned. Her name lives on as a cherished part of American history.

First Lady from 1817-1825

Elizabeth Monroe

June 30, 1768 - September 23, 1830

*During the last days of the French Revolution, Elizabeth made a
name for herself by her courageous visit to the imprisoned wife of the
Marquis de Lafayette*

Elizabeth Monroe

A quiet, elegant, accomplished woman, Elizabeth Monroe quickly found herself the subject of criticism following James Monroe's inauguration as the fifth president of the United State in 1817. Her critics accused her of being snobbish, unaware of her earlier achievements and that she was a woman of proven bravery who had played a courageous part in an uneasy moment of European history. Her demeanour could have been attributed to poor health rather than the unsocial apathy of which she was accused, though the Washington elite were perhaps too disappointed, following the excitement of Dolley Madison's tenure, to define a reason for her manner.

Elizabeth was the second of the five children of a Dutch sea captain, Lawrence Kortright, and Hannah Aspinwall. She was brought up in a wealthy background, her father having made his fortune as a merchant. He had also been a privateer in the British army during the French-Indian War. She was one of four privileged girls, all of whom had debuts, though Elizabeth was the darling of the society set. She and her sisters travelled throughout Europe. It is assumed that the girls received the customary education befitting a daughter of an affluent family, and in later years, Elizabeth became fluent in the French language.

It was at a dazzling social function that Elizabeth met the delegate to the Continental Congress from Virginia, James Monroe, who was ten years her senior. She was a self-confident, stately, handsome girl, who quickly caught James' eye. A lawyer, James was a quiet, dignified man, tall, well made, and known for his honesty, which was clearly expressed in the frank honest expression of his face and eyes. Almost from the start, he nicknamed Elizabeth his "Smiling Little Venus." Elizabeth's family did not fully approve of James as they felt he was not of the same social circle, but despite family reservation, they married in February 1786, shortly before Elizabeth's eighteenth birthday. The couple moved to James' native Virginia, where he maintained a law practice. They eventually moved to Charlottesville to be near their close friend, Thomas Jefferson, and produced three children. Their only son, James Spence, died in early infancy. Their two pretty daughters, Eliza and Maria, were destined to play a notable part in their mother's future.

A strong advocate of Jefferson's policies, James was elected to the Senate in 1790, but even though the family home was in Philadelphia, Elizabeth spent much of her time with her sisters in New York. In 1794, she was delighted when her husband was appointed as the ambassador to France, and she happily moved with him to Paris. The family arrived there during the latter part of the French Revolution, and they found the beautiful city in turmoil, with over a hundred officials having been guillotined five days prior to their arrival. In spite of this, Elizabeth became fond of the city and its people, who responded well to the family. Recognising the importance Parisians placed upon personal appearance, social behaviour, and culture, Elizabeth cultivated a persona that embodied casual American custom, but also respected European protocol. She embraced French fashions and trends, and her delicate beauty won the hearts of the French, who named her "La Belle Americaine."

James and Elizabeth enjoyed the French artistic and literary life and were charmed by the attention of orchestras that invariably struck up "Yankee Doodle Dandy" whenever the couple entered a theatre. The Monroes were so determined to integrate into French society that the whole family learned to speak fluent French. Elizabeth gained a reputation for the hostess skills she carried out in spite of deprivations resulting from the revolution. However, although she made all visitors welcome within her home, she refused to accept the protocol of returning the courtesy visits of diplomatic wives. This created a backlash of resentment against Elizabeth but did not deter her from the decision. Enthusiastic about decorative arts and furniture, Elizabeth purchased items to enhance their living quarters, and eventually she and James introduced the best of French art to the United States.

The excellent relationships James had with ministers and diplomats, and the dignified manner of the whole Monroe family, assured a number of European governments that the United States was a powerful, sophisticated, democratic new nation. Elizabeth took care never to offer political opinions, though she was once placed in an unwelcome political spotlight. Adrienne Lafayette, wife of the Marquis de Lafayette (a great friend of George Washington), had been imprisoned with her mother and grandmother, who had been taken to the guillotine. Madame Lafayette lived in daily fear that she would soon be marched off to the same fate. George Washington wished for her release as did James Monroe and many ideas were considered about how this could be achieved diplomatically. Elizabeth's popularity with the adoring hordes that followed her around whenever she left home in her well-known carriage sparked one idea. If "La Belle Americaine" visited Madame Lafayette in prison, would this generate public sympathy for the prisoner through Elizabeth's ardent supporters, who would surely follow her journey to the jail? With considerable misgivings, Elizabeth agreed to try this. It was arranged that she and servants would travel by carriage through the Paris streets. The anticipated crowds soon gathered and followed her toward the prison. The intrigued crowds increased as word got around about her obvious destination. When she arrived, Elizabeth asked in a clear voice to speak to Madame Lafayette. Knowing who Elizabeth was, warders brought the terrified prisoner to her.

Madame Lafayette, who perhaps had thought she had been summonsed to the guillotine, collapsed into Elizabeth's arms in copious tears. As the two women embraced, Elizabeth whispered words of comfort as she tried to console her. This moving scene impressed the crowds and word spread about the poignant meeting of the two ladies—one ashen and ill, clad in prison clothes, and the other beautiful and proud, though exuding compassion for her friend's plight. Shortly afterwards, James Monroe and the French government held talks and Adrienne Lafayette was released on January 22, 1795.

The outcome of another intervention was not as successful. While in Paris, the prominent American writer, Thomas Paine, had publicly declared strong opposition to the execution of King Louis XVI, and he was imprisoned by the French government. With great diplomatic skill, James Monroe eventually secured Paine's freedom and later hosted him in his home, where Paine castigated the Americans for allowing him to stay in a French prison for so long. This verbal attack within the Monroe home was reported back to America, and the incident, together with Monroe's lavish praise of France that contradicted the strict U.S. neutrality policy, led to Monroe's recall.

James returned to a political career in Virginia, where he was elected governor in 1799 for four years. During these years, Elizabeth suffered the deaths of her father and only son, and she developed serious health problems. Symptoms described by contemporaries suggest that the illness may have been a type of epilepsy, which in later years often left her shaking or falling into unconsciousness.

During his years in France, James Monroe displayed strong sympathies for the French cause, and in 1803, he returned to Paris, accompanied by Elizabeth, where he and Robert R. Livingston helped to negotiate the purchase of

Louisiana with Napoleon. The public was delighted to see the return of "La Belle Americaine." Following this, James was appointed as ambassador to London, where society tended to treat the couple with disdain. At that time, the British could not understand the U.S. refusal to engage as an ally to either France or England and alluded to a perception that their country was a parvenu in the world of nations. Thus, the status of the unhappy American ambassador and his wife was undermined, and their stay in London proved difficult. They returned to the U.S. in 1807.

In 1811, James was appointed as secretary of state in President Madison's administration. By then, Elizabeth had experienced moving within the highest political and social circles of Europe and America, and her hostess skills had been honed to a high standard. However, her health had deteriorated further, and she preferred to reside in Virginia with her daughters. During her infrequent trips to Washington, she rarely attended official functions or reciprocated social visits, and her reputation for snobbery began. The reputation intensified when James was nominated as the Republican choice for president, and with little Federalist opposition, he easily won the 1816 election. Elizabeth did not participate in the campaign or attend his inauguration ceremony. She was not even present at the inaugural reception, even though it was held within their home because of the ongoing White House renovations following the 1814 fire.

Her continued long absences from Washington meant that the president himself was left with much of the detail in running the White House. This led to a minor scandal when public money appeared to have been mishandled over the purchase of new furniture. An investigation concluded that the president had not personally been involved, but the episode had seriously embarrassed him. Many believed that if his wife had been available to oversee such matters, the president would not have been caught up in the issue.

During the following months, her husband undertook a goodwill tour, and in Boston, his new administration was hailed as an "Era of Good Feelings." However, these sentiments would not endure as Elizabeth refused, just as she had done in France, to return social calls or visit diplomatic wives and other officials. Elizabeth's elder daughter, Eliza, had married George Hay, a prominent Virginian lawyer in 1808, whose claim to fame was as the prosecutor of former vice president Aaron Burr for treason. Eliza, depicted as a haughty, pompous socialite, quick to remind others of her good breeding and lofty station, frequently substituted for her mother as the White House hostess. It was she who slowly changed the mood and aura of the White House. Many accused her of attempting to create the formal ambience of European royal courts. Despite her apparent conceit and aloofness, however, Eliza earned respect for her work with the victims of the fever epidemic which struck Washington during the Monroe administration.

Washington society and the president's administration were so concerned about the social changes that James was obliged to call special cabinet meetings to explain them (in December 1817 and September 1819). It was decided that because the First Lady was unable to participate in all of her formal social duties, the organisation of departmental social events, dinners, and other activities would henceforth become the responsibility of each individual department. This was a good time for the state of Elizabeth's health to be made known to the cabinet, a measure strongly advocated by Louisa Adams, the wife of the secretary of state, who knew Elizabeth well. In those days, however, it was not considered morally correct to discuss a lady in public, though Louisa felt that the president should present the reasons for Elizabeth's nonparticipation in the privacy of a cabinet meeting. The president did not believe he could, or should, do so, and an opportunity to vindicate his wife was missed. Had the diplomats' wives been made aware of her health problems and of her service in France in previous years, it is conceivable that they may have been more tolerant toward her.

When their younger daughter, Maria, married her first cousin, Samuel Gouverneur, in 1820, many Washingtonians had expected to be invited to this first presidential family wedding at the White House. Common sentiments were that the wedding would be a golden opportunity for the president and his wife to "build bridges." However, Elizabeth and Eliza insisted on a private ceremony and reception with only close family in attendance. There was continual friction between Eliza and Gouverneur, who served as the president's secretary, and eventually he and Maria moved to New York when he was appointed as the postmaster of New York City.

The administration and Washington society gradually, though reluctantly, accepted the changed social pattern, especially as Elizabeth and Eliza maintained the weekly

Drawing Rooms and the fortnightly formal receptions. One reception guest, Mrs. Edward Livingston, on being received by Elizabeth, wrote, "Mrs. Monroe looks more beautiful than any woman of her age I ever saw. She did the honours of the White House with perfect simplicity; nothing disturbed the composure of her manner." If Elizabeth could not attend one of these functions, Eliza substituted for her, and it was she who made sure the visiting schedule and the receiving of callers was severely curtailed.

James remained a popular president as he struggled with foreign affairs, particularly the threat of the more conservative governments in Europe, which he felt might try to aid Spain in winning back her former Latin American colonies. He was elected for a second term in 1820, and Elizabeth maintained her "aloofness" until he finally left office in 1825.

James received hearty cheers as he left the White House on his final day, though these became subdued as Elizabeth stepped into the carriage. As they commenced the long drive to their home in Oakhill, Virginia, on that day, Elizabeth may have been reflecting on the scenes of adulation as she left Paris so many years ago, contrasting them with the coolness of the American public towards her as she left the White House.

At home, out of the limelight, Elizabeth and James lived a quiet life. By then, Elizabeth was more prone to seizures as her general health continued to decline. During one episode, she fell unconscious into a fire, sustaining severe burns with resultant facial and neck scars. She took a long time to recover from this trauma and became more of a recluse (perhaps as a result of the scarring). She died in September 1830, at the age of sixty-three. James was devastated and inconsolable. In his misery, he robbed history of important information about Elizabeth when he burned all the correspondence and notes from their life together. He predicted that he would not live long after his wife's death, and he was proven right when he died ten months later, in July 1831.

First Lady from 1825-1829

ℒouisa ℋdams

Febuary 12, 1775 - May 15, 1852

*"There is something in this great unsocial house which depresses my
spirits beyond expression..."*

(Refering to the White House)

Louisa Adams

Louisa Adams was the wife of the sixth president of the U.S., John Quincy (JQ) Adams. She was also the daughter-in-law of the second president, John Adams, and his wife Abigail, but did not meet her in-laws until after the end of their term. She shared an immediate rapport with her father-in-law, though a mutual wariness between Louisa and her mother-in-law, was evident. It was obvious that Louisa's demeanour was unacceptable to Abigail, who did not like her "airs and graces."

By the time that JQ and Louisa entered the White House in 1825, Abigail was dead and unable to provide firsthand advice concerning Louisa's new role. Louisa actually hated the White House and wrote to a friend that "there is a spirit within this house that makes it impossible for me to feel at home." She was a shy woman who had been under the thumb of her domineering husband since her wedding day. She disliked the socialising expected of her as First Lady. She had little in common with JQ except a stubborn, short temper. Making a home for him had always proved difficult for her, and her apathy toward the White House put further strain on their relationship.

Louisa was an American citizen born in London in 1775. She was one of seven daughters of Joshua Johnson, the U.S. ambassador to Great Britain and an English woman, Catherine Nuth-Johnson. They also had one son, Thomas. Louisa's childhood was happy and carefree. "I was," she once wrote, "the first object of attention at home, every fault pardoned, every virtue loved."

Louisa's father was posted to Nantes, France, during the American Revolution, when Louisa was four-years-old. It was there that she received her main education at a convent school, and where she and JQ met for the first time as children. On the family's return to London, Louisa and her sisters presented as typical French girls in manners, dress, and language. Surrounded by tutors and governesses, they relearned English, and Louisa became a well-educated, pretty young woman. She was musical, bright, charming, and from a wealthy background, so it was not surprising that she had many beaux prior to meeting JQ again in 1794. By now, JQ was a twenty-seven-year-old diplomat to whom she was immediately attracted. They married in 1797, when she was twenty-one, the year her father-in-law began his term as the second U.S. president.

John's diplomatic career took the couple to Berlin soon after their wedding. Louisa displayed considerable flair and poise as a diplomat's wife and hostess, sustained by her education and background. She began to notice signs of her husband's self-absorption while in Berlin. Her marriage had not been easy from the beginning as JQ proved to be stern and dogmatic, not given to romance or affection. Louisa often resented his making family decisions without consulting her. He ignored any of her wishes that did not coincide with his, and expected Louisa to be subordinate at all times. She was sensitive, gregarious, and impulsive, and was often guilty of venting her anger in stormy scenes for which she would afterwards feel ashamed. She tried to understand her husband and made allowances for him. She knew, for instance, that he had had a love affair with Mary Frazer, a fourteen-year old American girl whom he had met as a young lawyer. He wished to marry her, but his mother soon put a stop to it, feeling that Mary was too young to settle. It broke his heart, and he withdrew into a shell, which even Louisa could not penetrate. She knew that his attraction to Mary had been far more intense than it was for her, but, in spite of that, she remained captivated by the ambitious diplomat.

JQ was also insensitive to her health. She had eleven pregnancies during their first twenty-one years of marriage. The first seven pregnancies had miscarried, which may have led to her eventual poor health and depression.

In 1801, the couple and their three-month-old son, George, moved to America. Louisa was a twenty-six-year-old mother, setting foot for the first time in the large country of which she had always been a legal citizen. She despaired that her European ways would never meet the requirements of her new environment. Louisa was dismayed at the American culture just as Abigail Adams despaired of her daughter-in-law's English ways. Her husband provided little support in her dilemma as he pursued his career. She visited her parents who had returned to America to live near Washington. They gradually helped Louisa to adapt to her country's ways. Even her mother-in-law tried to help, though her coolness was off-putting to the sensitive Louisa.

The years that followed were divided between their home in Quincy and houses in Boston and Washington. JQ had swiftly moved up the political ladder. During that period, she gave birth to two sons, John and Charles. In 1809, JQ was appointed as the first U.S. minister to Russia, and he and Louisa travelled to St. Petersburg, with their younger son, Charles. The older boys, George and John, remained with their paternal grandparents. Louisa had not been consulted about the decision to leave them behind. She was deeply shocked at her husband's duplicity in making the plans behind her back and that his parents had apparently agreed with JQ's decision. It was JQ's wish that his sons should be educated in America, and by the time she knew of his intention, it was too late for her to do anything about it. Louisa could hardly bear the sudden enforced separation, and depression dogged her throughout the long journey to Russia. Her sorrow eventually decreased as she began to receive letters from the boys.

In spite of her heartbreak over the absence of her sons, Louisa loved the glamour and pomp of the Russian court. However, she found the long, cold winters and the strange customs difficult to cope with. Their limited financial situation, which always undermined their marriage, was another source of trial as she tried to manage the household budget. She began to suffer stress headaches, eye trouble, and painful hands.

In 1811, she gave birth to a longed-for daughter who died twelve months later. Louisa's grief was overwhelming. She missed her older boys more than ever and lived for their letters. She gained some pleasure from tutoring her younger son, though her endeavours were often derided by JQ, which affected her self-esteem and confidence. That led to a deeper and more lasting depression. At last, her husband felt that he ought to do something to help. For a birthday present, he bought her the book "Treatise on Diseases of the Mind" by Benjamin Rush. As she read it, Louisa questioned her own sanity.

In 1814, JQ was called to Ghent to work on peace negotiations while his wife and son Charles remained in St. Petersburg. On completion of the Ghent assignment, JQ was called to Paris with no time to return to Russia. He wrote to Louisa and asked her to sell their property and join him in Paris as soon as possible. He charged her with making the sale and travel arrangements. Louisa exhibited much courage during that time. She sold their possessions, ensured that the cash was well-hidden, and made travel arrangements. She had grown fearful of the thousands of miles of war-ravaged territory across Europe and was nervous that Napoleon had escaped and was once more on the rampage. She was unable to persuade her servants to travel with her and she could only obtain the services of three unsavoury people. Louisa and Charles set off with those men on a forty-two-day journey, which she later described as "filled with danger, intrigue and even murder."

Roving bands of desperate stragglers and highwaymen filled her party with terror, and Louisa often feared for their lives. The three frightened servants left her one by one, but she overcame the tribulations courageously. She reached Paris safely, though her journey had left her tired and ill. When she summarised her ordeal to JQ, he did not concede that her trials had been unusual, nor did he acknowledge her bravery. She became even more depressed. When he later noted the reaction of his friends and family to her remarkable feat, he became suitably impressed and told her so.

In 1815, JQ was appointed as British ambassador in London. The two years there proved pleasant for Louisa. Not only was she in an environment which she knew, her two older boys had joined them, and the family enjoyed a peaceful life together. It was during that time that Louisa and JQ once again began to share their joint love of music.

JQ was appointed as James Monroe's secretary of state on their return to Washington at the end of 1816. Louisa's receptions proved successful, and she became popular with the diplomatic corp. Her "at home" evenings were boosted by classical music, and her lead in establishing theatre outings contributed to her success as a diplomatic hostess. Her most glittering triumph was a party which she organised for the returning hero of New Orleans, General Andrew Jackson. Over 800 guests attended the ball which was so successful that the National Intelligencer published a poem about it entitled "All Are Gone to Mrs. Adams." She still did not enjoy the enforced socialising and longed for more personal leisure time.

JQ was nominated as a candidate for the 1824 presidential election. He refused to campaign personally, believing in arrogance that the presidency was due to him for all his years of service to America. His sponsors and Louisa took on the essential task of cultivating his nomination. Louisa shared her husband's ambitions and worked energetically carrying out visits and attending dinners, balls, and receptions. She invited influential people to her receptions, and, for the first time in their marriage, Louisa found herself side-by-side with JQ as his campaign manager.

The 1824 presidential election was contentious, with four candidates from within the sectionalised Republican Party: John Quincy Adams, Andrew Jackson, William H. Crawford, and Henry Clay. The four men fought a hard battle with no outright winner, and members of the House of Representatives were left to make the decision. Henry Clay, who had received the least votes and had stood down, cast his crucial vote for Adams, thus, ensuring his election. Clay became Adams' secretary of state, leading to accusations of a "corrupt bargain." The enraged Andrew Jackson, who had actually received more popular and electoral votes than Adams, began a campaign for the 1828 elections almost at once.

Louisa's pride at her husband's achievement was tarnished by the accusations and her own ill health, as she constantly battled against deep depressions. As First Lady, she maintained the weekly "Drawing Room" events, though would have preferred to spend her evenings playing her harp or reading. During that time, she began to compose music and verse. She did not resurrect the visiting of diplomatic wives or the returning of social calls, which had been discontinued by her predecessor and friend, Elizabeth Monroe. As that change had now been fully accepted, Louisa did not suffer the venomous disparagement placed upon her predecessor with whom she had fully agreed on the issue.

Louisa did not entertain very much, but when she did she preferred the formal style of the Monroe's, though her parties tended to be more lavish, possibly because of her European background. She also preferred to greet her guests by mingling with them, going from group to group, rather than receiving them formally in line surrounded by cabinet wives. The highlights of her entertainment were her son's wedding and a birthday party for the Marquis de Lafayette, with whom she and her husband had maintained a strong friendship.

The presidency of JQ was a failure from the beginning, which exacerbated Louisa's depressions. His choice of Henry Clay for secretary of state was unpopular, and his plans for transportation, agriculture, education, and science were all rejected. In spite of the efforts of Louisa, many congressmen began to boycott the few events to which they were invited. The president and First Lady spent lonely evenings together in the White House during their isolated presidency. Louisa made several visits to spas to obtain relief from her ailments while her husband made regular, lonely visits to their home in Quincy.

Not surprisingly, JQ served only one term as president. During the 1828 election campaign, opponents charged him with corruption and public plunder, an ordeal which he and Louisa found hard to bear. Defeated by Jackson, the couple returned to Quincy, Massachusetts, once more uneasy in their relationship. It was the death of their elder son, George, in April 1829, which brought them closer. They drew comfort from each other in their deep sorrow. Louisa was then fifty-six and in her sadness was grateful to be in her own home instead of the White House. However, she was soon to become disillusioned about a longed-for peaceful retirement when her husband accepted an invitation to run for Congress. He won by a landslide and spent the rest of life working productively in the Lower House. Louisa began to play a part in his work as they both became drawn into the anti-slavery movement.

JQ was shocked at a rule that prevented the reception of anti-slavery petitions. It was known as the Gag Rule. JQ made it clear that he was a champion of the constitutional right of petition. In his efforts to rescind the Gag Rule, he found himself aligned with anti-slavery crusaders, which he had previously avoided. He worked hard for eight long years with Louisa's support. They used every means possible to have the rule repealed. They finally achieved it in 1844, and even JQ's political enemies were impressed.

By that time, both JQ and Louisa had developed good

relationships with abolitionist leaders, and JQ revised his opinions about rights for women. Louisa helped to sort out letters and petitions from slavery abolitionists, and it made a crusader out of her. Simultaneously, she had been going through the papers of her parents-in-law and JQ had become impressed by his mother's strictures against slavery and her insistent demands for improved legal rights for women. JQ realised that he had been so involved with his own career that he had never paid attention to his mother's perceptions. Louisa also recognized that she had never known the real Abigail Adams, and she grieved for the lost opportunities to be her friend and ally. Together, Louisa and JQ prepared pamphlets and books, organised conventions, and made public speeches on abolitionism and rights for women. The couple found as they did so that their marriage had finally become a rich one.

John Quincy had always been a workaholic, and Louisa had tried constantly to protect him from it without success, even in the closeness of their last years. Inevitably, his luck ran out and he collapsed from a stroke at his desk in the House of Representatives. Louisa was called and rushed to his side, but he never regained consciousness. He died two days later, on February 23, 1848, at the age of eighty-one.

Louisa suffered a stroke a year later, which partially paralyzed her left side and she died in Washington in May 1852, at the age of seventy-seven. Congress honoured her by adjourning for the funeral, which was attended by President Millard Fillmore and other officials. Louisa had finally been recognised for what she was: a courageous, intelligent, and true daughter of America.

Louisa and JQ are buried at the family church of Quincy. Theirs was not a sparkling marriage, though it was one of dedication, especially for Louisa. Had her mother-in-law, Abigail, been fully aware of the strengths Louisa had displayed in her departure from Russia and later in the abolitionist and Women's Rights movements, she would surely have been proud of her.

Phase Two

RELUCTANT FIRST LADIES

1829-1869

The Jackson Ladies

The Van Buren Ladies

Anna Tuthill Symmes Harrison

The Tyler Ladies

Sarah Polk

Margaret Mackall Smith Taylor

Abigail Powers Fillmore

Jane Pierce

Harriet Lane

Mary Todd Lincoln

Eliza McCardle Johnson

Reluctant First Ladies

If the first forty years of the American presidency had seen the development of the First Lady role, the following forty years yielded a pattern which could have led to its possible demise.

The period from 1829 to 1869 was a strange era as far as the First Lady role was concerned. Of the eleven presidencies, only three First Ladies, Sarah Polk, Harriet Lane, and Mary Lincoln, completed their full tenure without pleading illness or infirmity, or obtaining a substitute to carry out their role.

Three presidents had legitimate reasons for asking young relatives to carry out these duties (widowers Andrew Jackson and Martin van Buren and bachelor James Buchanan).

John Tyler introduced his daughter-in-law, Priscilla, as a substitute at the request of his invalid wife, and his younger daughter, Letitia, stood in when Priscilla and her husband moved away. His second wife, Julia, became First Lady for the last few months of his second term.

The wives of Presidents Taylor, Fillmore, and Johnson claimed illness or infirmity and appointed substitutes to carry out their White House duties, and the substitute for William Harrison's ailing wife did not get into her stride at all, as Harrison died within a month of his inauguration.

The 1820s had brought about an insidious change to the procedures for highlighting those who might, one day, achieve a senior political office. By 1829, qualifications for voting included all adult white males, rather than just property owners. Deference was no longer paid to the more wealthy, educated, and professional candidates. An appeal to a Convention of Party delegates for nomination to Congress had superseded the party caucus, and nominations were considered from all backgrounds.

What of the ladies of this new brand of candidate, however? Wives of the "old-style" congressman would have received extensive training in household management, etiquette, and personal presentation. A number had the benefit of moving in European royal circles as well as extensive travel, making them well able to host a reception or run a political household. Most of the wives of "new-style" congressmen, however, would not have received the level of education deemed essential to carrying out their role as a Congress wife, and were looked down upon by a snobbish group of old-Washington residents, whose word appeared irrefutable as they reigned supreme. This inflexible group regarded all congressmen and their families as a "floating" population, not worthy of their best attention. There were women, already exhausted by bearing and rearing children, struggling to carry out yet another enervating role for their political husbands. Doubtless, they would rather have relinquished their new role than risk rebuke or denigration from this seemingly spiteful group.

One of the first casualties of this culture appears to have been Rachel Jackson, who died just weeks after the election of her husband, Andrew, as president. Her story of heartbreak and despondency during this period, as the socialites reproved her previous marital history, is as distressing today as it must have been to her husband's friends and followers then. Even her sudden death, which many blamed openly on the attitude and adverse behaviour toward her, did little to prevent "floaters" from receiving continuous verbal assaults and gossip from the socialites. Whether they felt remorse at the way they treated Rachel Jackson is not known. What is recognised is that Washingtonians were delighted with her niece, Emily Donelson, a pretty twenty year old with a simple, pleasant manner, who was popular as Jackson's hostess, and acknowledged as the unofficial First Lady of his presidency. Emily was similar to her Aunt Rachel in many ways, with little education and travel experience to boast about, but her youthful face and figure in the Washington social whirl was a great success.

When Martin Van Buren became president (1837–41), his daughter-in-law, Angelica, became his hostess. The socialites took the shy, nervous young woman to their hearts, and gradually, she grew into the role, becoming a popular, elegant hostess who exerted real influence.

William Harrison died within a month of his inauguration, and his daughter-in-law Jane Harrison, who had stood in for Harrison's sickly wife, had no opportunity to make any positive impact.

Zachary Taylor, who followed President Harrison, died in office within sixteen months of becoming president. His daughter, Betty Bliss, affectionately known as "Miss Betty," became extremely popular as the young substitute for Taylor's ailing wife, Margaret (Smith) Taylor, who was a woman of high character though failing health. Once again, the Washingtonians accepted another enthusiastic, bright young paragon of efficiency and charm with obvious enjoyment.

Abigail Powers Fillmore, a teacher, had met her husband, Millard, when he was working as an indentured farming servant and had worked with him for many years, helping to improve his education. Prior to his election as the thirteenth president, Abigail became partially lame following an accident and was housebound, in constant pain. In spite of her frail health and lameness, she supported her husband's elevation to the presidency and served as the White House hostess. However, her continuing frail health eventually led to the transfer of her duties to their nineteen-year-old daughter, Mary.

Jane Pierce, the frail wife of Franklin Pierce, had a history of illness throughout adulthood. By the time she entered the White House as First Lady, her physical and mental health had deteriorated further, resulting from the loss of her three sons, the last one in an accident just prior to Franklin's inauguration. The public were sympathetic toward their new president and his wife, but expectations were that they would overcome their personal grief in order to fulfil their national duties. Jane was unable to do so and a relative occasionally acted as her understudy. Society accepted this, now well used to substitutes. Jane remained secluded from the public eye as much as possible, and the public eventually tired of a First Lady who attended only a few receptions and did not receive or return calls. The White House remained a dismal establishment during the Pierce presidency.

Harriet Lane, a niece of bachelor James Buchanan, was designated as his First Lady at the age of twenty-seven. Highly educated and sophisticated, with an authoritative air, she carried out her role with diplomacy and dignity. She did not suffer from the socialites' gossip, but even had they been against her, she would have turned her renowned diplomacy to resolving any differences. While history includes Harriet in the list of "youthful First Ladies and substitutes," she was clearly not a substitute, and it was rumoured that she exerted great influence over the president. A cheerful person to have around the White House with an astute sense of decorum, fashion, and conversation, she used her position to promote American fine art and was a proven campaigner.

Andrew Johnson had been so concerned at the adverse reaction of the fabled Washington socialites towards President Lincoln's wife that he worried about the effect the group might have on his ailing wife, Eliza. It was agreed that their daughter, Martha, would assume the general household duties at the White House, aided by her widowed sister, Mary. Eliza stayed in her room for most of the time, but remained mentally active and kept a careful eye on political issues so that she and Andrew could enjoy intelligent conversations at the end of each day. It was conceded that Eliza's legendary influence over her husband endured, while others openly commented that the First Lady had retired behind the cloak of illness in order to escape unwanted social duties. History reveals these views to be unjust and a sad reflection on the misconceptions that were allowed to develop in the era.

The use of relatives in the cases of widowers Andrew Jackson, Martin van Buren, and bachelor James Buchanan was not remarkable and easily accepted, and it was within an unusual but understandable set of circumstances that three young women served in the First Lady arena during President John Tyler's term of office.

It would have been a curious era indeed had it not been for Sarah Polk and Mary Lincoln, the only two wives of presidents who had fully retained their First Lady positions. Both were ambitious and intelligent women with good educational backgrounds, each with many years of experience preparing them for their position. The difference between the two was Sarah Polk's unswerving dedication to her husband's career, while no one was ever sure of Mary Lincoln's commitment to anything except her own need for personal recognition.

Sarah Polk stood out as a dedicated First Lady in a period when others had been almost invisible. Often likened to Abigail Adams in her approach, Sarah's excellent health, inquiring educated mind, and her childlessness helped her to devote her full time to her husband's career and health. While there was speculation that Sarah controlled her husband, she rarely received the accusations of interference that had besieged Abigail Adams. When she and her husband left the White House in 1849, Sarah's popularity was high, with press reports indicating that it had been hard to fault this feminine, well-dressed First Lady. According to the press, it was obvious that she had appealed to those who had wanted an intelligent, reasoning woman in the White House, a far cry from Abigail's departure. Was it Sarah's better education and their contrasting approaches—careful reasoning against excessive frankness, diplomacy against tactlessness—that made the difference?

In an era which was pointing toward a possible subversion of the traditional First Lady role, Sarah Polk was an icon, but Mary Lincoln's celebrity was very different. There was as much unfounded animosity toward her political allegiance during the war-torn years as there was toward her personality. The entrenched Washingtonians played an infamous part in the misery of this matronly lady. For a time, Mary retreated out of the sight of staff and the public, just as some of her predecessors had done. In time, however, Mary rallied and, spurning the secretary of state's offer to host a major event in honour of Prince Napoleon, she made all the arrangements for the successful event. It was felt then that if Mary had paid as much attention to supporting her husband as she had to that occasion, she may have succeeded in disarming his critics, but having returned to the fold, she badgered and hindered him. She lobbied on behalf of favour-seekers and there was concern that the president was always ready to acquiesce to her requests. It is not recorded whether this readiness was to prevent further verbal onslaught, though a perceptive observer may be forgiven for pondering on that possibility.

Yet, for all her faults, Mary Lincoln showed a kind of courage and determination, particularly in her refusal to renounce her role as First Lady. Indeed, of all the First Ladies within this unusual era, Mary was one who had cause to plead grief in order to avoid the undoubted stress she was under. She stubbornly refused to take this way out. If only she had harnessed this courage and her energy toward more constructive outlets, there may well have been a different outcome to her life.

The appointment of substitutes during these four decades had been an obvious and practical solution to individual dilemmas. It is not difficult to discern that the public liking and acceptance of youthful substitutes may have become a prop upon which some reluctant First Ladies had learned to lean upon in order to avoid some of their unpleasant duties and encounters. However, while Mary Lincoln had done little for the cause of the First Lady role and was definitely not the best example of an emerging "new woman," she did help, along with Sarah Polk and Harriet Lane, to break the pattern of invisible, weak First Ladies.

Died prior to Andrew Jackson's 1829 inauguration

Rachel Jackson

June 1767 - December 22, 1828

"I am glad of it for Mr. Jackson's sake for it is his ambition... for me it is one more burden."

(On hearing about her husband's election as President)

Rachel Donelson Robard Jackson

EMILY DONELSON
(Niece of Rachel Jackson)

SARAH YORKE JACKSON
(daughter-in-law of Andrew Jackson)

Rachel Jackson's friends found her weeping copiously and hysterically in a reception room of a Nashville newspaper office on a December afternoon in 1828. She was the wife of Andrew Jackson, president-elect of the United States. The newspaper's editor was a relative on whom she had called after a shopping trip. There, she had rested and waited for friends to take her back to the Hermitage, her nearby home. Large, uncontrollable tears ran down her ashen face, and she could not speak for a time. A friend discovered a crumpled campaign leaflet thrown into a corner. It was the leaflet that had stunned Rachel.

The leaflet clearly defended her against venomous slander. Until that moment, she had not realised the lengths to which her husband's adversaries had gone to disparage the couple, and Rachel, in particular. The verbal and written attacks were begun in February 1827 by Thomas D. Arnold, and had been mostly kept from her. Rachel, who had not wanted her husband to stand for president in the first place, was shocked and mortified at the viciousness of the propaganda. She knew that there had been talk about her marriage, though not to the extent revealed to her by that leaflet.

Rachel was the youngest of eleven children. She was born in June 1767 as the fourth daughter of John and Rachel Stockley Donelson. Her parents were both of long-established English stock. John Donelson was a surveyor and citizen of Chatham, Virginia. He served for several years in the House of Burgess. In 1779, James Robertson persuaded him to join a venture to found a settlement in the Cumberland Basin of Tennessee. Donelson found himself leading a party of about one hundred and fifty people over a long, dangerous road and river journey, eventually settling in the Cumberland River area. Coping with heavy floods and attacks from the Indian population, they moved three times before finally settling. Defeat of the Indians eventually ensured the steady development of Nashborough (later to become Nashville), where Donelson and Robertson became highly respected within the settlement.

The families who had made the arduous journey had little time for formal education and etiquette as new settlers. Communal education was scant though Rachel's parents did teach their children basic reading and writing. Rachel would always regret her lack of formal education.

Little else is known of Rachel's early life. A gregarious, buxom beauty, she met and married Kentucky landowner, Lewis Robard, when she was seventeen. The two were totally unsuited to each other and their marriage was unhappy from the start. Rachel was a lively and fun-loving girl. As such, she found it difficult to please Robard, who beat her and accused her of being unfaithful when other men showed an interest in her. Rachel reassured him that there was no cause for his misguided jealousy, but after many rows, he ejected her from the home they shared with his mother, who strongly protested against his treatment of her daughter-in-law. Rachel returned to live with her widowed mother, who now ran a boarding house. Within weeks, Robard wrote to his wife that he could not live without her, and he begged for reconciliation. Rachel agreed, and he joined her in Nashville.

Around 1788, a dynamic young lawyer named Andrew Jackson came to lodge at her mother's boarding house. He was considerably taken with the good-looking Rachel, who reciprocated his friendly attention, incurring the wrath of her husband. Robard loudly broadcast his suspicions, stating that Jackson was too intimate with his wife. A furious Andrew took him aside and threatened that he would cut off his ears if Robard ever connected his name with Rachel in that way again. Andrew added with such vehemence that he was tempted to carry out the threat anyway that the scared Robard had a peace warrant sworn against him. The magistrates dismissed it when Robard suddenly left the area.

He returned, however, and there was a further skirmish between the two men. Andrew had been anxious about the troubles he had inadvertently caused Rachel, and he sought out the returned Robard and once again denied any wrongdoing. The men quarrelled violently, and Robard threatened a whipping. Andrew accepted the fight, citing "gentlemanly satisfaction." The quarrel ended when Robard returned rapidly to Kentucky, vowing in a torrent of profanity that he would never see Rachel again. Andrew found it expedient to find lodgings elsewhere.

In 1790, Rachel heard that Robard was returning to Nashville with plans to take his wife back to Kentucky, by force, if necessary. It was hurriedly decided that Rachel should travel to relatives in Natchez in the company of a family friend, Colonel Robert Stack. Andrew volunteered to go along with them "in case of Indian attacks." Rachel arrived safely, and Andrew returned to Nashville with Colonel Stark to continue his successful law career.

In December 1790, Robard secured a document from the Virginia legislature permitting him to sue for divorce. Waiting a few months until he assumed that a divorce had been granted, Andrew rode to Natchez, where he and Rachel underwent a marriage ceremony in August 1791. They returned to Tennessee in October of that year and purchased a farm near the Donelson plantation. It turned out that Andrew had misinterpreted the details of the act permitting divorce proceedings. Two years later, he received devastating news. Due to Robard's slapdash approach to the legal issues, he had not achieved his divorce until September 27, 1793. Andrew and Rachel found it hard to believe that their marriage was invalid and that Rachel was guilty of adultery and bigamy. They would not accept it until legal friends persuaded them to remarry, which they did on January 17, 1794. They settled down again as embellished stories of their plight inevitably became the talk of the county. Such talk would follow them for the rest of their lives.

Over the years, the reckless, headstrong Andrew had fought a number of duels whenever he heard untoward comments regarding Rachel's honour. He actually killed one protagonist, Charles Dickinson, in Kentucky in 1806. The fact that Andrew felt compelled to undertake such duels gradually mellowed the normally effervescent Jacksons. Rachel became devoutly religious while the impulsive Andrew became thoughtful. He respected his wife's deep religious views. Many questions remained over their tumultuous marriage, but their Tennessee neighbours accepted the couple as a respectable and happily married couple. One of their neighbours, Andrew B. Lewis, once wrote, "The General and Mrs. Jackson both perhaps acted imprudently but no one believes they acted criminally. The whole course of their lives contradicts such an idea." Their love endured through all the gossip and scandal. Andrew prospered as a lawyer, merchant, and planter, and later, as a soldier.

In 1804, the couple moved to their house, the Hermitage, which Rachel loved. They were childless, though the large new home was always filled with children. A year earlier, Andrew's friend Edward Butler had died, naming him as guardian of his two sons. In 1805, Rachel's brother Samuel died and his three sons went to live at the Hermitage. One of those boys, Andrew Jackson Donelson, would eventually become Andrew's presidential private secretary. In 1810, they legally adopted one of the twin sons of another of Rachel's brothers, who was treated in every respect as their son. Rachel was a kindly, maternal woman, well loved by all the boys. She liked to relax with a pipe at the end of each busy day. She smoked in contentment on her porch, as many frontier women did.

During the 1812 war, Andrew won fame as an ardent fighter against the Indians in the defence of New Orleans. Rachel managed the family and their home, while writing constant affectionate letters to Andrew. His military career continued during further campaigns against the Seminole Indians. In 1821, he was appointed as governor of Florida for four months. Rachel accompanied him to Pensacola, where she became active in the strict enforcement of the Sabbath observance laws.

Following the military campaigns and the short stint in Florida, they returned to the Hermitage in Nashville to live a gentle life. Their peace did not last. Andrew's political career had taken off, and in 1824, he was nominated for president, much to Rachel's disquiet. He lost to John Quincy Adams following an extremely dirty campaign but was nominated again in 1828. The second campaign became an even more unscrupulous fight. Andrew's opponents depicted him as an immoral home-wrecker. They used even more loathsome aspersions against Rachel through leaflets, handbills, and the newspapers which championed Adams for a second term. The cruel comments of the press cited the guilty verdict of an eminent Tennessee committee which had conducted an investigation into the charges of wilful immorality by Jackson and his wife. The newspapers supporting Andrew Jackson insisted that the professed impartial results were unfounded.

Andrew found the vilification to be one of the main battles of his campaign, along with ensuring that his wife did not become aware of the worst of the odious gossip. Despite the rancour, however, Andrew won the election. When Rachel heard the results, she said, "Well, for Mr. Jackson's sake, I am glad; for my own part, I never wished it."

While Rachel had not been aware of the savagery of the campaign against her, she had known that stories were circulating. Through it all she had remained charming, affable, and kind, in spite of the conclusions of a segment of Washington society that she was not fit to serve as the nation's hostess. Having lived briefly in Washington, she had already been involved with that critical bunch of established Washingtonians. She had been the object of gossip and rancour even then. They had mocked her lack of etiquette and finesse, her unfashionable, rustic appearance, her obvious lack of education, and that she had not travelled, was not a good conversationalist, and was obese. They laughed, above all, at her pipe-smoking habit. Worst of all, they criticised her alleged adultery and bigamy without knowledge of the full facts. All the rumours and the last dirty campaign had deflated her spirit and personal confidence. Beaten down by the turmoil, she began to suffer bouts of palpitations and difficulty in breathing.

Rachel did not wish to attend Andrew's inauguration. She wanted to slip into Washington unobtrusively after the event. However, Andrew's friend, Senator John Eaton, strongly recommended that she should be at the ceremony. Rachel reflected on what he said, but remained uncertain.

She eventually gave way when Eaton said, "If you shall be absent, how great will be the disappointment. Your persecutors may then chuckle and say that they have driven you from the field of your husband's honours." Rachel began making arrangements for the ceremony and asked the help of friends in the design of her inauguration dress.

Two weeks after the printing shop revelation, Rachel was taken ill and Andrew hurried from Washington to be with her. She rallied slightly on his arrival but died shortly afterward on December 22, 1828. Andrew was distraught. He was convinced that the strain of the campaign and the personal attacks on his wife had taken her life. He proclaimed such loudly at her funeral on Christmas Eve at the Hermitage, where thousands of shocked people had flocked and where Andrew wept openly. Rachel was shrouded in her inauguration gown and was interred in the garden of her beloved home. Later, Andrew built a limestone temple resembling a Greek gazebo over her grave. Whenever he returned to Nashville, he visited the temple daily.

Andrew entered the White House as a widow in March 1829. He had appointed Andrew John Donelson, Rachel's nephew, as his private secretary, and asked Donelson's wife, Emily, to perform the hostess duties. Emily took on the role at only twenty-one-years old, skilfully combining the care of her husband and child with her hostess duties. She would eventually give birth to three more children in the White House. Perhaps because she was so young and capable, she proved to be popular among the diplomats and socialites. She is listed as the official First Lady of the United States from March 4, 1829 to December 19, 1836.

Emily's father was Rachel Jackson's brother, who ran a farm in Donelson, Tennessee, where Emily grew up. She was educated at Nashville Female Academy and was considered to be bright and accomplished. She married her first cousin (known within the family as JA), on September 16, 1824. She had willingly agreed to take on the White House hostess duties for the sake of her aunt, of whom she had been very fond.

A mourning period was imposed during the first months of the Jackson presidency, when a number of receptions and engagements were curtailed, allowing Emily to ease her way into her new role. She was assisted by her husband, as President Jackson, a sad and lonely man, continued to grieve for his wife. The mourning period was deemed to be over when the traditional presidential New Year's Eve party was held in 1829, successfully organised and hosted by Emily. During the months prior to that event, Emily had strengthened her reputation for efficiency and charm and the Washington society who had so cruelly castigated her aunt Rachel, accepted the likeable and endearing young woman as the nation's hostess.

The relationship between the president and Emily did not flourish, however. Emily had become irritated with the stance taken by the president toward the recent marriage of John Henry Eaton, the secretary of war. Rumours were rife that the marriage had followed an extramarital relationship that had resulted in the suicide of Peggy Eaton's first husband.

The scandal, known as the "Petticoat" affair, split the cabinet as Vice President John Calhoun publicly snubbed the couple. Others refused to receive Peggy into society. President Jackson felt that this behaviour was unfair and indefensible, resembling it to the treatment of his late wife, while Emily agreed with the faction that snubbed Peggy. However, when the president pressured her into inviting Mrs. Eaton to White House events, she relented, though extended only rudimentary courtesies to her. When Eaton declined a personal invitation to a White House dinner, the president asked him why. He was appalled when he heard that it was due to the First Lady's coldness toward Mrs. Eaton. A conflict grew between the president and Emily, ending with Emily's defection to her mother's home in the summer of 1830. When her husband and the president returned to Washington following a short vacation there, Emily refused to return so long as the president insisted upon Peggy Eaton's acceptance into the White House. The estrangement and the "Petticoat" affair lasted for over a year and it was eased only when the president dismissed several members of his cabinet and posted John Henry Eaton to Madrid, as America's minister to Spain. The main reason for their alienation removed, Emily returned to the White House in September 1831.

During the summer of 1834, Emily began to feel unwell and both her husband and the president became anxious about her. Sarah Yorke Jackson, the wife of Jackson's adopted son, was recruited to act as a co-hostess, which helped Emily tremendously as she struggled to cope with her hostess duties and growing family. While Emily remained the formal

White House hostess, Sarah became known as "mistress of the Hermitage" (Jackson's home.) Emily and Sarah worked well together without friction. This unusual job-sharing created history, as it was the first and only time that two women worked simultaneously as the White House hostess. Emily's health began to decline, however, and in 1835 she was diagnosed with tuberculosis. She left the White House in June 1836, in order to recuperate at the plantation adjacent to the Hermitage (Tulip Grove.) It was there that she died in December 1836, at the age of twenty-nine. Sarah Jackson presided over the White House for the last few months of her father-in-law's tenure.

When Andrew Jackson moved back to the Hermitage, Sarah, her husband, and their five children, went with him, where they continued to live until his death. Following his death they found the maintenance of such a large plantation to be onerous and moved to Mississippi prior to the Civil War, leaving the plantation in the care of their slaves. It was eventually purchased by the State of Tennessee and is now a museum. Sarah died in August 1887.

When Andrew had returned to he Hermitage, he reflected on a promise he had made to Rachel years earlier. It was on a Sunday in 1823, as they walked to church, that Rachel had, for the umpteenth time, asked him to join her church. "If I were to do that now, it would be said all over the country that I had done it for the sake of political effect. My enemies would all say so. I promise you that when I am clear of politics, I will join the church," he told her. He knew that she had looked forward to it, and he kept the promise when he joined the Presbyterian Church.

Andrew Jackson died in 1845 and was buried next to his beloved Rachel under the Greek gazebo. His personal story is often forgotten. People remember only the so-called scandal of his marriage. However, Rachel knew him as an important leader of men whose steadfastness against the British in the War of 1812 had earned him the nicknames of Old Hickory and Old Hero. She knew him as an oppressor of the Indians and as the recognized hero of the 1815 Battle of New Orleans. She never knew of his fight against Southern sedition during his presidency or of his determination to keep the Union together. As president, he had met the threat with the strength he had shown as a military leader and with the subtlety he had gained as a politician. He had not had his precious wife at his side, but he knew that she would have been proud of him.

Hannah Van Buren
March 8, 1783 - Febuary 5, 1819

Angelica Van Buren
Febuary 13, 1816 - December 29, 1877

Hannah Van Buren died following childbirth 18 years before her husband became President in 1837. Her son's wife, Angelica, was appointed as the White House Hostess. Both women are included in the First Lady biographies.

The Van Buren Ladies

HANNAH HOES VAN BUREN
(wife of President Van Buren)

ANGELICA SINGLETON VAN BUREN
(daughter-in-law)

Martin Van Buren had been a widower for eighteen years when he moved into the White House in 1837. Unlike Thomas Jefferson and his immediate predecessor, Andrew Jackson, both widowed prior to becoming president, Martin had neither daughter nor daughter-in-law, or any other suitable relative, who could act as his hostess. His four bachelor sons had moved with him to the White House with no indication of any pending marriages. Van Buren felt, however, that there was no need for an official hostess and that he would not require such support.

Van Buren's wife, Hannah (Hoes), had died at the age of thirty-six in 1819. She was Martin's cousin, hailing from a close-knit Dutch family. The two had grown up together and attended the same village school in Kinderhook, New York. Her niece has recorded that she was a woman of "loving, gentle disposition" and "of modest, even timid, manner." Church records indicate her formal affiliation to the church, which she apparently considered of great importance. She was twenty-three years old when she married Martin, who was twenty-four and who had wanted to postpone their marriage until he had established a successful law practice. The first of five sons was born in Kinderhook, and she gave birth to three more sons in Hudson, though one died in early infancy.

As Martin's law practice prospered, he became involved in New York politics. Within a year of their marriage, the couple moved to Hudson where Martin served as county surrogate and continued his political interests, eventually becoming the leader of the Albany Regency, a powerful New York political organisation. Hannah joined and fully supported the Presbyterian Church. The family moved to Albany in 1817, and Martin served as state attorney. Their fifth son was born in 1817. Hannah became a staunch supporter of a Sunday school championed by John Chester of the Albany Presbyterian Church. The main work of the school was to teach the unlettered waifs of the street to read. Hannah believed strongly in the enterprise and, disregarding the majority of the church women who were against it, threw herself into the work. It was during their first harsh winter in Albany that Hannah developed tuberculosis, and she died in 1819.

Hannah had been aware that she was dying and had made it known that she would like the money normally given by the family to the pallbearers to be donated to the poor. That and her work with the Sunday school ensured she would be remembered by the people of Albany as a woman of compassion. Her gravestone states, "She was a sincere Christian, dutiful child, tender mother, affectionate wife." As it was not considered seemly for a gentleman to "shame" his wife by ot included in her husband's biography. Therefore, there is little further information about her personality and life, a loss to the history of the era.

Stricken after the loss of his wife whom he had known all of his life, the small, trim, and smartly dressed Van Buren put his whole ego into politics and was elected to the United States Senate in 1821. By 1827, he emerged as the principal northern leader for President Jackson, who appointed him as secretary of state and later became Jackson's most trusted adviser. So little is known about Hannah's thoughts, personality, or attitude towards politics that it is not easy to speculate how she would have felt about her husband's success, especially when he was elected president in 1836.

If Hannah had lived and moved to the White House, she would no doubt have had the same reservations as her husband and sons as they entered the mansion, which had been rendered shabby following the extensive public use of the building during the Jackson era. Used to living in elegant style, Martin and his sons set about refurbishing their new home immediately.

The president felt confident that he could cope without a formal hostess, particularly as a former First Lady, Dolley Madison, who lived in nearby Lafayette Square, often visited and presented him with plenty of advice. On one of these occasions she brought a distant relative from South Carolina, Angelica Singleton. Angelica was a handsome, well-educated young woman with aristocratic manners, and it was not long before she won the heart of Martin's elder son, Abraham. They married in November 1838.

Since Abraham was his father's secretary, Angelica was expected to undertake the duties of First Lady. By that time, the president had realised the need for an official hostess, just as Jefferson came to that realisation thirty-six years prior. The Washingtonians welcomed the good-looking and effervescent young girl, and she became a popular, successful hostess. She carried out her duties gently and competently under the guidance of her husband and Dolley Madison. However, her impact was not always positive. She was inclined to behave in a condescending manner as if she were at a European royal court, and she preferred to sit on a dais, surrounded by a court (usually young girls of her age) at her receptions. This tendency ruffled quite a few feathers, but the matronly socialites tended to forgive and forget, putting her behaviour down to youthful uncertainty.

Angelica presided over an uneasy house as the financial panic of 1837 that had begun during the Jackson presidency struck a severe blow to the prosperity of America. Jackson's destruction of the Second Bank of the United States had removed restrictions on some of the banks and there was wide speculation in land and properties, based on easy bank credit. In an effort to stem this speculation, Jackson had issued a "Specie Circular" requiring that land must be purchased with gold or silver (hard money). The panic began early in Van Buren's presidency, when hundred of banks and businesses failed, and for five years, the United States was overcome by the worst depression thus far in its history. Van

Buren declared that the panic was due to the over-expansion of credit and recklessness in business matters, and he devoted his efforts to ensuring the solvency of the country. He did not rescind Jackson's deflationary policies, however, and history reveals this actually prolonged and even deepened the depression. He opposed the expansion of slavery and consequently blocked the annexation of Texas (which he felt would add to slave territory). As a lonely man, he must have wished for the comfort of his wife to help him bear the stress and strains of the situation.

The Whigs defeated him in the 1840 elections. When he retired from the presidency a few months later, he left a far more elegant White House and another unnoticed legacy. The Washington socialites and general public had again accepted a pretty, youthful hostess who was not a presidential wife as the national hostess. Along with Emily Donelson (President Andrew Jackson's niece), Angelica Van Buren can be credited for having played an important part in that development.

First Lady March 1841

Anna Harrison

July 25, 1775 - Febuary 25, 1864

"We are here for four years. I do not look beyond that, as many things may occur during that time..."

Anna Tuthill Symmes Harrison

JANE HARRISON
(daughter-in-law)

When William Henry Harrison was elected as the ninth president in 1840, his wife's reaction was similar to that of Rachel Jackson's twelve years earlier. "I wish that my husband's friends had left him where he is, happy and contented in retirement."

There are other parallels with Mrs. Jackson. Anna had always hoped her husband would finally settle as a gentleman farmer. He did for a while but was always pulled back into national affairs. Like Jackson, he spent much of his time away from home and, as Rachel Jackson had done, Anna managed the household in her husband's absences. Both women were devout, stoically accepted "God's will," and found solace in religion during the hardships of life.

Following a stormy election campaign, William was inaugurated as president at the age of sixty-eight in 1841. His wife was an ailing woman of sixty-five and on the advice of her doctor did not travel to Washington for the inauguration. She planned to travel in the spring of 1841, thus, avoiding the harsh Washington winter. It was arranged that their widowed daughter-in-law, Jane Harrison, would carry out the First Lady's duties until her arrival.

Anna was the second daughter of a New Jersey judge, John Cleves Symmes, and Anna (Tuthill) Symmes. Her paternal ancestors had settled in New Jersey in the early seventeenth century, eventually migrating to Long Island, where Anna was born on July 25, 1775. Her mother died a few months following her birth, after which Judge Symmes and his daughters returned to New Jersey where he became fully committed to wartime duties as a militia colonel. When Anna was almost four years old, she was sent to her maternal grandparents in Southold, where she stayed until she was eighteen years old in a happy though restricted Presbyterian household. Recognising her academic abilities, her grandparents placed her in the Clinton Academy in East Hampton and later in the renowned Isabella Marshall Graham School in New York, where she completed her formal education. At home, under the guidance of her grandmother, she received intensive religious and domestic instruction.

As Anna matured into an educated, accomplished woman, her father's career also progressed. He held a number of public offices in New Jersey, served as a representative in Congress, and became an associate Supreme Court judge. When the Northwest Territory opened, Symmes was astute enough to purchase a large area of land from Congress, and by 1789, had founded the frontier community of North Bend on the Ohio River.

By that time, his second wife had died and he returned

to Southold, where he met and married Susanna Livingston. He took Susanna and his daughter, Anna, of whom he was very proud, to Ohio. Anna's older sister had married Philip Shorten, and the party stopped off at their home in Lexington, Kentucky, en route. There, Anna met William Henry Harrison, a handsome, experienced soldier of twenty-two and of impeccable Virginian heritage, and he became the love of her life. However, Judge Symmes disapproved strongly of their relationship, not wishing the hard life of frontier forts for his beautiful, talented daughter. He also objected to the fact that William, charming and educated as he was, had only a small inherited fortune, with no profession or prospects other than the army. Despite her father's objections, Anna was determined to marry William and after many quarrels with her father, the couple married in November 1795 in the home of the local justice of the peace, Dr. Stephen Wood, though Judge Symmes did not attend. It would be fifteen years before Anna's father would accept the marriage, which he often referred to as "rather a runaway match." As he mellowed and could see the happiness of the couple, he finally relented and regarded his son-in-law with some affection.

Although a confident woman, Anna remained a quiet, modest figure and was a devoted, loyal wife and mother to their nine children (a tenth child had died in infancy) throughout her husband's consequent public service as the first governor of Indiana Territory (1800–1812), state legislator, U.S. congressman, senator, and minister to Columbia. She was an impeccable and dignified hostess, fulfilling the obligations that her husband's various positions required of her. However, she had no real taste for the formal social life imposed upon her, instead, preferring the company of her husband and children.

Anna accepted William's long absences with resilience and understanding, but she welcomed the eleven quiet years from 1829 to 1840 in North Bend, where they finally settled. That peace was dashed when he was nominated by the Whig Party to stand for the president in the 1840 election, which he won. During the inauguration ceremony, William broke an oft-quoted record when his 8,500 word inauguration speech lasted over two hours. The weather had been severe that day, and the cold was ferocious in its intensity as he stood without coat or hat, so it was not surprising that the new president suffered a bad cold almost immediately following the ceremony. On a bright April morning in 1841, as Anna was reluctantly packing for her journey east, she received the shocking news from Washington that her husband had died from pneumonia on his thirty-second day in office. Traumatised at the suddenness of this tragedy, she mourned with dignity and bravery and her religion sustained her throughout.

Anna mourned her husband for the rest of her life, which she spent in North Bend, receiving comfort from her family, neighbours, and religion. Congress awarded her with the first year's salary of her husband, amounting to $25,000, the first pension ever paid to a First Lady. She remained in their marital home until a fire destroyed it in 1858, after which she moved to the nearby farm of her son, John Scott Harrison.

Her grandson, Benjamin (John's son), would eventually become the twenty-third president.

Anna's deep religious fervour strengthened over the years following William's death and the deaths of eight of her children, the only one to survive her being John. As her own health deteriorated, she maintained a pious life and was a firm supporter of her Presbyterian church. She died at the age of eighty-eight in 1864. Almost the whole population of North Bend turned out for the funeral, and many felt that the Reverend Horace Bushnell's eulogy, based on the theme of "Be Still and Know I Am God," was very apt for their gentle neighbour. She was buried beside her husband in the North Bend Harrison tomb on a headland overlooking the Ohio River.

Unwittingly, Anna Harrison had created a number of historic "firsts." She was the first ever First Lady to have received a formal education, the first who had never lived in the White House, and the first (and to date the only one) to have been the First Lady for only one month, the first to receive a government pension, and the first to be a grandmother of a president.

First Lady from April 1841 - September 1842

Letitia Tyler

November 12 1790 - September 10, 1842

"Whether I float or sink in the stream of fortune, I shall never cease to love you"

(letter from her husband)

The Tyler Ladies

LETITIA CHRISTIAN TYLER (first wife)

PRISCILLA COOPER TYLER (daughter-in-law)

LETITIA "LETTY" TYLER SEMPLE (daughter)

JULIA GARDINER TYLER (second wife)

LETITIA TYLER

John Tyler took an oath of office on April 6, 1841, following the untimely death of President William Harrison. He became the first vice president to take over the role of president of the United States. His wife, Letitia Christian Tyler, became the First Lady, although a reluctant one.

She was recovering from a paralysing stroke that had left her an invalid with limited movement, although her general health had improved and she was able to manage her home. When John became the president unexpectedly, he wished her to be with him at the White House. At first she refused, but gradually, as her condition stabilised, she travelled to Washington. Letitia was able to play a significant role in household activities, which she directed from her suite of rooms where she lived in semi-seclusion, and while she managed the domestic arrangements, her daughter-in-law, Priscilla, the wife of her son Robert, undertook the hostess role.

Letitia received invited guests into her rooms while Priscilla attended the official dinners, receptions, and Drawing Rooms. Reports from such visitors confirmed that while she was frail in body, Letitia retained a high interest in current topics, which she apparently discussed with John at the end of each day. She took an interest in charities, especially those for children and education. She often donated to them from her own limited purse and occasionally allowed her name to be used in appropriate and non-controversial fund-raising.

The general public never saw the First Lady and neither did the Washington sociality. They were all agog to meet the mysterious Mrs. Tyler, but Letitia made only one public appearance at the White House wedding of her daughter, Elizabeth, in January 1842.

She was born in November 1790 to Robert and Mary Christian at the Cedar Grove plantation in New Kent County. She was the seventh of twelve children. Her wealthy father was from a prominent Virginian family with Federalist leanings. Little is known of her early life until her meeting with John Tyler, a law student from Richmond. They were good friends for a while, and eventually, their friendship blossomed into romance. During their quiet, somewhat undemonstrative courtship, John poured out his love in sonnets and elegantly worded love letters to her. On one occasion, Letitia expressed surprise at his words, to which he replied in a letter, "To ensure your happiness is now my only objective. Whether I float or sink in the stream of fortune, you may be assured of this, that I shall never cease to love you."

They married on March 29, 1831, five years after meeting.

That same year John was elected to the Virginia House of Delegates. In 1825, he was elected as governor of Virginia after having served two terms in Congress. Two years later, he returned to Washington as a senator. He resigned in 1836, having become opposed to the Republicans and Party leaders in Virginia.

John's political career grew as his family increased. Letitia, a woman of tranquil beauty and fair complexion, bore nine children over the years, two of whom died in infancy. She was modest and demure throughout their marriage. She was more submissive than John would have wished, but she preferred to be seen as her husband's homemaker, caring for the family's needs, sewing, knitting, entertaining their friends and neighbours. When John first went to Washington, she demurred at following him, stating that she should be at home with her children.

Years later, her daughter Mary spoke of how her mother had taught her and her siblings to read and write out of the Bible and she recalled how Letitia was often found seated in her large armchair, a small stand at her side, which held the only books she ever read—her Bible and prayer book. There was only one occasion on record when Letitia asserted herself. John was considering sending Mary to a school run by nuns in Georgetown, but Letitia put her foot down firmly. She said that she did not wish for a catholic education for her children. She ensured that Mary went to a Williamsburg school.

President John Tyler may have been unprepared for the subsequent tumult he underwent by being plunged so suddenly into the president's seat. By August 1841, his administration was in turmoil. During that month, John had vetoed a bank bill, which led to protests for two nights. A rowdy, frightening mob surrounded the White House, waving fire torches, banging drums, blowing horns, and burning an effigy of the president. The protest and the nagging worry of a continual drain on their family finances led to the deterioration in Letitia's health. She suffered a second stroke in September 1842 from which she died. Letitita was the first wife of a president to die in the White House. Politics and rancour were put aside for a while as the Tyler family and the whole nation mourned the First Lady. Even the National Intelligencer, an ardent critic of the Tyler administration, paid tribute to her qualities as a good wife and mother.

Letitia was interred in the family plot at Cedar Grove, the town where she was born fifty-two years earlier. Though President Tyler married again, he never forgot the first love of his life.

PRISCILLA COOPER TYLER

Priscilla Cooper Tyler, the wife of the president's son Robert, undertook the full role of First Lady when her mother-in-law died. As she lay dying, Letitia had asked Priscilla if she would fulfil the role. Priscilla, though nervous, vowed that she would do anything for her mother-in-law whom she loved dearly. It was Letitia who had welcomed her into the family on her marriage to Robert and treated her with respect as a well-loved daughter. Letitia's generous support boosted Priscilla's confidence and made her understand that her former acting profession was not detrimental to her life in a prominent political family. Once, when visitors had covertly sneered at Priscilla's former profession, Letitia sent them packing and would not admit them again to her home.

Priscilla was the third child of the Irishman Thomas Apthorpe Cooper. He was a well-known, favourite actor of the American stage for thirty years. He had been brought up by the political philosopher, William Godwin, and had emigrated from England at the age of twenty-two. Godwin had inspired him by extolling the principles of freedom, which Cooper passed on to his children. His beliefs were so intense that in later years he built a separate house for the children and their governesses, next to his own in Bristol, Pennsylvania.

His second wife, Mary Fairlie (Priscilla's mother), had been a witty, beautiful darling of New York society. Her pleasant manner inspired visitors to call at their home (including Napoleon's brother, Joseph, and Washington Irving). When Priscilla was about fourteen years old, it was Irving who wrote of her that although she was talented, she was incapable of application and that she had not a single accomplishment. He could not know that one day she would fulfil one of the most important tasks in the land.

Priscilla's mother persuaded her daughter to join her father's theatrical company in 1833. She was not beautiful, but she had a pretty, piquant face and others felt that her vivaciousness would make her a success. The audiences loved her, praising her sunny countenance and beautiful golden hair. However, Priscilla had no inclination to work as an actress and ended her career five years later, described by the Knickerbocker magazine as but a "bud of promise." By then she had met Robert Tyler, a tall, distinguished-looking man, who had fallen in love with her while watching her play Desdemona in Othello performed in Williamsburg.

Robert and Priscilla married in September 1839. They lived in Williamsburg, where he worked as a lawyer. She assisted him where she could and helped to write his court speeches, but she was concerned and disappointed when Robert gave up his practice to help his father as a vice-presidential candidate in 1840. However, she threw herself wholeheartedly into the campaign and was eventually supportive of Robert's decision to change his career.

When she accepted the role of First Lady, she was aware of the guidance available from a former First Lady, Dolley Madison, and from the secretary of state, Daniel Webster, and with their help rose to the occasion. She was praised by Washington society, who enjoyed the freshness of a youthful hostess. Her personal beauty blossomed, her confidence grew, and she became a witty, sparkling conversationalist.

The most notable event of her tenure was when she accompanied the president on an official tour of the United States in the summer of 1843. This created an unprecedented level of publicity for both. Priscilla's reputation as First Lady had preceded her, and she received much media and public attention. It was not seen as good etiquette in those days for ladies to be mentioned by name in the press. Priscilla's impact was so profound,however, that her name was frequently used in the news.

Letitia Christian, Priscilla's second child, was born in the White House shortly before the tour. The little girl had brought great joy into her parent's lives and was the impetus for Robert to think about his future career. Robert and Priscilla had also heard rumours of a romance between the president and Julia Gardiner, though they never discussed it. In March 1844, Robert resigned from his White House post and joined a law firm in Philadelphia. They were devastated when their first child died in 1845, followed by the death of a son, John, soon after his birth. Priscilla bore four more daughters over the years. Her last child, Thomas, died in early infancy.

During the Civil War, Robert, who was a Southern supporter, fled to Virginia where he was joined by Priscilla and the family. He served the Confederacy in civilian and military matters, while Priscilla and the children spent much of their time at the home of her sister, Mary Race Raoul, in Richmond. They settled in Montgomery when the hostilities ended. Robert became the editor of The Advertiser. When he died in 1877, Priscilla remained in Montgomery, where she died in 1889 at the age of seventy-three.

When Priscilla left the White House, her sister-in-law, Letitia (Letty), took over her duties, though not with the same panache. Letty was glad of advice from Dolley Madison, who persuaded her to reinstate social calls to the White House, thus restoring Dolley's former custom. Letty enjoyed her new way of life, and she and her sister Elizabeth devoted themselves to this duty on three afternoons a week, pleasing both socialites and diplomatic wives. She was shocked and resentful when she learned three months after taking on the role that her father had married Julia Gardiner, and she left the White House in a great huff. Letty later divorced her husband, James, and lived a miserly life, running a school for girls. She forever refused help from, and reconciliation with, her father, and never spoke to him or Julia again. Many years later, she returned to the White House as a friend of future First Ladies Lucy Hayes and Ida McKinley, fully accepted by the Washington socialites.

JULIA GARDINER TYLER

Julia Tyler was thrust into the nation's limelight at age twenty-four, following her marriage to the president in June 1844. She had unimpeachable social credentials, having been born into high rank. She carried out the role of First Lady with poise. In mourning for her father, she tended to dress in either white satin, black lace, or royal purple, but she brought a youthful style and vivacity to the White House.

Julia was charismatic and gregarious, and she revelled in being the centre of things. She soon charmed society with her excellent education and conversational expertise. One of the first issues she tackled was a thorough cleaning of the

White House, which she felt had become a dirty establishment. Within weeks, the mansion was described as a sparkling place.

The splendour of events at the White House became the talk of Washington. Julia introduced the polka and waltz, though she would only dance herself if she could open the ball with her husband. Julia was always conscious of the impact she made in the limelight. She initiated the playing of "Hail to the Chief" whenever the president appeared in public and demanded the announcement of names on arrival at receptions, where she mingled with eminent Americans and foreign visitors with easy grace. She also reinstated the former visiting schedules after listening to guidance from Dolley Madison.

The only criticism held against her was that she behaved at times in a queenly manner, putting on airs and graces and being altogether too courtly. The social elite, thrilled with another young, brilliant hostess, put this down to the arrogance of her youth and forgave her indiscretion. The newspapers called her "Lady Presidentess," since the term "First Lady" had not yet been accepted. A New York musician composed the "Julia Waltzes" in her honour, and John Tyler was very proud of his lovely young wife.

Julia was a good-looking girl with dark hair, huge grey eyes, and a slender, shapely figure. She had an impulsive, often reckless nature. She had been a trial to her staid parents, Senator David Gardiner and his wife Julia. When their daughter was only nineteen years old, she consented (without permission from her parents), to allow her image to be used for a store advertisement, thus, becoming known as "The Rose of Long Island." Her furious parents whisked her off to Europe in an attempt to overcome their shame, where she had many suitors. She was presented to King Louis-Philippe and Queen Marie and became infatuated with royal courts while meeting other royal personages.

On return to the United States, Julia and her sister Margaret took New York by storm. The girls attended receptions at the White House and were introduced to the president in 1842. During this time, Julia received proposals of marriage from two congressmen and a Supreme Court judge. The president himself appeared to be smitten, and he invited Julia and her family to the White House on Christmas Eve, 1843. By the following February, gossips were making much of the friendship between Senator Gardiner's daughter and the president. The social whirl ended abruptly on February 28, 1844.

A presidential cruise had been arranged on the gunboat, USS Princeton. The president and his secretary of state, John Mason, together with cabinet members and friends, including Senator Gardiner and his daughters, were all on board. As they passed Mount Vernon, the former home of George Washington, a gun salute was fired. The secretary of state, Senator Gardiner, and six others were killed in an explosion caused by one of the guns backfiring.

Julia fainted when she heard that her father had been killed. A story followed that the president carried the stricken young woman down the gangplank when the Princeton docked at Alexandria. Julia had dearly loved her father, and his death was the greatest shock of her life. After his death, she spent more time with the president and she mentioned to friends that no man other than the president could fill the void her father had left. No engagement was announced because of the mourning period for her father and John Mason. President Tyler married Julia at the Church of Ascension on Gardiner's Island amid great secrecy on June 26, 1844. After breakfasting with friends at the Gardiner home, the couple returned to the White House for a large wedding reception.

John Tyler was the first president to marry while in office. The media was taken completely by surprise. They loved the romantic story and made the most of it. Although there were many articles, jokes, and talks about the thirty-three-year age difference, it was clear that Julia loved her husband dearly.

John had become subdued during his first wife's long illness. His natural humour emerged once more, influenced by Julia. He did not object to her hiring a New York reporter, whose task was to provide favourable coverage of the Tyler family. He did, however, censure her blatant nepotism as she lobbied for patronage of her brothers. All in all, he found that his wife was a considerable asset.

As a New Yorker married to a Virginian, Julia listened to her husband's views and took them seriously. She lobbied for the annexation of Texas. John signed the joint congressional resolution for the annexation as Julia watched at his side, three days before leaving office in 1845. Afterwards, he presented her with the pen he had used to sign the historic document, and she later turned the pen into an elegant necklace, wearing it with pride on appropriate occasions.

John and Julia left the White House in February 1845, following a successful valedictory ball, opened by Julia. It ended with the ladies dancing a cotillion with ambassadors from Austria, Prussia, and Russia. On the day they left the White House, staff, guests, and ambassadors formed two lines to say a somewhat tearful farewell. They were all going to miss "Miss Julia."

Julia was twenty-five when she left the White House for John's extensive wheat and corn plantation he called Sherwood Forest. It was situated near Richmond, Virginia, and it was here that she gave birth to their seven children (five boys and two girls) between the years 1846 to 1860. She visited various health spas between the births of the children and always took with her an extensive and expensive wardrobe. As the mistress of Sherwood Forest, which had seventy slaves, Julia continued her renowned entertaining. Their marriage remained a happy, fulfilling one, in spite of financial concerns as a result of John's imprudent loans to family and friends, and Julia's high spending on entertainment and the high cost of her clothes.

Julia agreed with her husband on the rights of the states concerning slavery, and she encouraged her sons to support the Confederates and the Confederate Army. She spoke strongly on the subject when the publication of Uncle Tom's

Cabin inspired a letter from her to the Southern Literary Messenger, in which she lauded the plantation system and rejected the pleas of British women to help end slavery. The resulting attention created predictable adverse publicity, though many agreed with her. She was also an advocate of secession and had welcomed her husband's election to the Confederate Congress in 1861. When John died a year later, at the age of seventy-one, Julia was understandably distraught.

She was very aware of the potential dangers of Sherwood Forest being so near to the battleground as war loomed, and she decided to move her family to her mother's home in Staten Island, New York. She became heavily involved in the local pro-Confederate activities once she had settled. This antagonised her brother, David Lyon Gardiner, who was a loyal Unionist, and a rift formed within her family, which widened after her mother's death. The resultant inheritance struggle led to the celebrated case of Tyler vs. Gardiner (1864–68), creating a permanent family estrangement, though Julia eventually received a three-eighth share of her mother's fortune.

Following the Civil War, Julia fought another battle to restore to her the Sherwood Forest plantation, which had been overtaken by the Unionist Army and left in a damaged, battered condition. The long financial depression added to Julia's woes as she struggled to rehabilitate her home and settle her husband's numerous debts. She was bowed down by these financial struggles and the death of her daughter, Julia Tyler Spencer, in 1871, due to childbirth complications.

Using the title "Mrs. Ex-president Tyler," Julia put all her energy into lobbying, along with others, for a federal pension for presidential widows. An annual grant of $5,000 was finally announced in 1882, and this sum greatly assisted Julia's precarious financial position.

In 1872, Julia left the Presbyterian Church to become an Episcopalian and later converted to Roman Catholicism, an event widely heralded by that church. Her final years were spent in contentment and comfort in Richmond, where she died on July 10, 1889, at the age of sixty-nine, of a cerebral haemorrhage. She was buried next to her husband in the Hollywood Cemetery, Richmond, after a funeral mass at St. Peter's Cathedral.

First Lady from 1845-1849

𝒮𝒶𝓇𝒶𝒽 𝒫𝑜𝓁𝓀

September 4, 1803 - August 14, 1891

"If I get into the White House, I will neither keep house nor make butter"

Sarah Childress Polk

James K. Polk was always ambitious. He eventually became the eleventh president of the United States. When he was approaching thirty, he served as a clerk in the Tennessee legislature but felt his career was moving too slowly. He asked his friend, Andrew Jackson (who became the seventh president), how he could succeed in politics.

"You must settle down as a sober, married man," Jackson told him. James was unimpressed, but Jackson persisted, advising him that he needed to choose carefully, and that his future wife should be someone with wealth, family, education, health, and good looks. James Polk knew of such a woman, Sarah Childress.

Sarah Childress was born in 1803 near Murfreesboro, Tennessee, the third of four children. Her father, John Childress, a native of Campbell County, Virginia, settled in Tennessee in the 1790s, and became a prosperous businessman and politician. He often entertained General Andrew Jackson and other prominent persons during sessions of the

Tennessee legislature. Thus, Sarah and her siblings were brought up in the upper stratum of society.

Recognising the intellectual abilities of all their children, Sarah's parents ensured a fuller education for their two daughters than girls in the early nineteenth century normally received. In their early years, the girls had private tuition of a teacher from the Murfreesboro Boys' Academy attended by their brothers. When she was thirteen, Sarah was sent for a season to the Female Academy conducted by the Moravians in Salem, North Carolina, a prominent school for girls. It was there that the Presbyterian Church became extremely important to her and her devout religious beliefs developed. Unfortunately, she was called home before completing her course because of the illness and eventual death of her father, though by that time, she had already acquired an unusually fulfilled academic education. Her father was a wealthy man. He left a healthy estate, though during the 1819 financial panic, much of his wealth was lost due to poor management by the executor.

Sarah Childress first met James Polk when he was a student at the Murfreesboro Academy. They did not become well acquainted until years later, when he became a clerk of the state senate in her hometown. Each found the other's intellect and mutual interest in politics a huge attraction. Her black, curly hair, beautiful tailored dress, and light-heartedness relieved her plain features, and everyone she met found her impossible to dislike. James knew that the well educated, confident girl, used to the trappings of wealth and high culture, together with an ability to converse and socialise with important people, would be a good wife for him. He made the wise decision to court Sarah, which she welcomed. When he proposed marriage, she did not accept immediately. She told him that she would marry him on condition that he ran for state legislature before they married. That was the push he needed, so he agreed. They worked together during the election campaign, which he eventually won.

James and Sarah married on January 1, 1824. They rented a two-room log house in Columbia, which Sarah adored. She said that it was too small to be burdensome. She took a keen interest in politics and worked well with her husband as his career prospered. In 1825, he was elected to Congress, where he served for fourteen years, the last four as Speaker of the House. Sarah's social graces were honed in official circles as she gained popularity as a hostess.

The couple remained childless, which Sarah had resigned herself to, though she had dreamed of becoming a mother. During an era when housewifery and motherhood were a woman's only acknowledged careers, Sarah sought scope for her astute mind. She eschewed housekeeping and accompanied her husband whenever she could. She became heavily involved in the social whirl, though her strict Presbyterian upbringing precluded her from attending the popular horse race parties of that era. Neither would she attend a theatre. She was careful, however, not to upset the nurturing of social contacts that could be of future value to her husband.

In spite of the socialising, Sarah became bored and lonely. She assisted James in the writing of his speeches, copying his correspondence, and undertaking general administrative tasks. Her main desire in doing the work was to prevent her perfectionist husband from overworking. She would read out newspaper articles or circle them for his future reading, always leaving an appropriate comment, and it was not long before James found her indispensable. He trusted her judgement and asked her to review and analyse important documents.

Sarah continued to use her social skills to good effect, and she gained many loyal female friends along the way, usually academics or achievers and even wives of her husband's opponents. Her circle of friends also included prominent men, among them Andrew Jackson, Franklin Pierce, and Justice Joseph Story. Known to them as Betty, her friends valued Sarah's education, abilities, and discernment.

In 1839, James stood for Tennessee state governor, and Sarah worked discreetly with his closest advisors during the campaign. He won the race, though he lost the next two bids. Sarah worried about the effect of the hard campaigns on his health, though he never slowed down.

James suddenly found himself as the Democrat choice for president in 1844. There had been discreet enquiries by the Tennessee delegation as to the suitability of Sarah, the result of which sealed the nomination. James won the race for president, though lost his home state by 267 votes.

While James encountered hostilities during his administration, Sarah was impressive. Her social graces, appearance, and long-term Washington experience made her a perfect

First Lady, and she was warmly praised, even by her husband's opponents. Their joint reputation of never speaking ill of anyone, even the bitterest enemies, allowed Sarah to mix freely with the diplomatic families from both Whig and Democrat parties. For once, the Washington elite found little to criticise, except for Sarah's insistence on strict Sabbath observance in the White House, which included the banning of visitors on Sunday. She also imposed an unpopular ban on dancing and wine at presidential functions and attempted, without success, to forbid the playing of "Hail to the Chief." When Sarah realised that her strict religious austerity might damage her husband's standing, the suppression of Sunday visitors and dancing was withdrawn, though the policy of staff attending Sunday church services remained, and wine was allowed only sparingly at official functions. Sarah herself refused to dance at White House events, and whenever she attended a function, all dancing would stop until she left.

Sarah was aware of her lack of traditional beauty, so she always ensured that her personal presentation was impeccable. She was a handsome woman, with black hair and dark eyes which reminded one English visitor to the White House, who was impressed by Sarah's appearance, of an Italian donna. Sarah's intellect and talent for conversation also ensured that she remained highly popular. As the press became increasingly aware of the role of First Lady, she became the subject of newspaper reports, praising her deportment and general demeanour, though Sarah did not welcome such reports.

During James' presidency, Sarah continued to provide him with intellectual support and tried to sustain her most challenging task of keeping her husband from overwork. In this regard, she met with only limited success. It was for those reasons that Sarah was pleased to leave the White House at the end of the presidential term in 1849. The couple were greeted and cheered by large gatherings of well-wishers as they left the mansion for the last time and throughout their journey to their home, Polk's Place, in Nashville. James had planned a trip to Europe, and together, they made plans for the trip as they made their long journey home. They did not encounter problems until they reached New Orleans, where there was word of a cholera outbreak. Since the outbreak had probably originated and spread on shipping vessels, their proposed sea journey was cancelled. They continued by road, which considerably lengthened their journey. Upon arrival in Nashville, a tired James attended a rally organised in his honour, but worn out from his travels, he stayed only long enough to address the congregation. He collapsed when he arrived home.

His health deteriorated during the next few weeks, and their longed-for European trip was cancelled. Just three months after leaving office, James Polk died on June 15, 1849, and Sarah was guilt ridden, fearing that overwork was the cause of his sudden death. She felt she had failed in her most important task.

A widow at forty-six, Sarah's grief even overtook her religion for a time, though she later became more devout than she had ever been. She erected a marble tomb for James on the front lawn of their home and maintained a shrine within his study. Polk's Place was eventually converted to a museum in remembrance of her husband.

Sarah had asked her husband's niece and husband to live with her, together with their daughter, Saidee, of whom Sarah became particularly fond. Friends called upon her frequently, though she never returned their calls. Indeed, she never went out except to go to church. She remained positive throughout the years and kept her mind alert by expertly managing a prosperous thousand-acre cotton farm in Mississippi as an absent owner. James had acquired the farm prior to leaving the White House, which provided an adequate living for Sarah and her family. Her husband had recommended in his will that the plantation slaves be freed upon his death, but Sarah never got around to it, though she had always ensured that they were not abused in any way. It took the Civil War to free them.

Over the years Sarah became a national monument. It seemed that every prominent person or group visiting Nashville would stop and pay her respect. While it might have appeared so to others, it did not seem strange to Sarah that she would entertain a Confederate general at her home one day and extend the same courtesy to the Union forces on another. Brought up in the South, her sympathies were with the Confederates, though as a former First Lady, she had tried to rise above fragmentation. In 1891, she told an interviewer, "When it came to actual conflict, and the lives of people with whom I lived, and whose ways were my ways, my sympathies were with them: but my sympathies did not involve my principles. I have always belonged, and do now belong to the whole country."

She survived James by forty-three years. She died in August 1891 at the age of eighty-eight and was buried in the vault she had erected at Polk's Place. Later, her tomb was removed to the grounds of the Tennessee state capitol.

First Lady from March 1849 - July 1850

Margaret Taylor

September 21, 1788 - August 14, 1852

*After praying earnestly for her husband, Zachary Taylor, to lose the
1848 election, Margaret Taylor viewed a life in Washington with horror*

Margaret (Peggy) Mackall Smith Taylor

MARGARET (BETTY) BLISS
(daughter)

Margaret(Peggy) Mackall Smith Taylor was distraught. "It is a plot," she cried, "a plot to deprive me of his society and shorten his life by unnecessary care and responsibility." In November 1848, Peggy had just heard of the nomination of her husband, Zachary Taylor, for president. She calmed down when she realised his excitement at the prospect. She respected his eagerness and even took pleasure when he won the election. It soon became clear, however, that Peggy was ill-equipped for such a prominent position as First Lady, and she was reluctant to undertake the role.

Peggy was born in Calvert County, Maryland, in September 1788, the youngest of seven children. Her father, Major Walter Smith, had served in the Continental Army during the American Revolution and later became a prosperous tobacco planter. Her mother, Ann Mackall Smith, was one of the well-known "eight beautiful daughters of General Mackall." Peggy was related to a number of politically powerful families, including that of Robert Bowie, the three-time governor of Maryland.

Little is known of the early life of Peggy and her siblings, apart from the information gleaned from records of Nelly Custis, the granddaughter of Martha Washington. These records suggest that Peggy and her sisters socialised with Nelly and other prominent Virginian families. They probably received the practical education common in those days for daughters of affluent families.

There is one anecdote which is significant. Peggy and her family were eating supper one evening when she was about fourteen. Two young men appeared at their door seeking directions. The men, one of whom was Zachary Taylor, explained that they were travelling to Washington to seek a commission in the U.S. Army. Major Smith invited them to take supper with them. During the evening, the family were entertained with stories of Western frontier life. As it grew dark, Zachary and his friend were asked to stay overnight. While helping to prepare their accommodation, Peggy noticed Zachary had a severe limp. He explained that the cause was friction on an old arrow wound during his hard ride that day. Peggy insisted on treating and bandaging the lesion, which was significantly better the following morning. Zachary remarked to his friend that Peggy was a "dear girl." His friend responded by saying that she would "likely grow into a dearer woman."

Peggy's father died when she was sixteen. She moved to Louisville, Kentucky, to live with her married sister. Within five years of moving there, Peggy, now a pretty, laughing young woman, renewed her acquaintance with Zachary Taylor, who had become a lieutenant in the U.S. Army. There was immediate rapport between the two, and romance blossomed. Peggy was twenty-one and Zachary twenty-five when they married in her sister's log house on June 21, 1810.

The setting of the wedding was appropriate, as Peggy was destined to spend the next forty years in log cabins, crude army barracks, and sometimes in canvas tents. She had begun her married life by stating firmly that she would always remain at her husband's side while she remained in good health, regardless of deprivation. She endured hardship, danger, and privations within remote army camps in Indiana, Minnesota, Wisconsin, Florida, and Arkansas, as her husband slowly rose in rank. Zachary eventually became a major general in the Mexican War (1845–1847). She loved her itinerant life, so long as she could be with her husband.

Peggy bore five daughters and one son, Richard, who was born in 1826. He would eventually become a lieutenant general in the Confederate Army. One of the major tragedies of Peggy's life was the loss of two daughters (Octavia, aged three, and Margaret, aged one), in the 1820 fever epidemic. She was devastated at the loss, and she suffered delicate health from then on.

When their youngest children, Margaret (Betty) and Richard (Dick), were born in 1824 and 1826 respectively, Peggy watched their health carefully. She insisted that they should be raised in a more civilised way than her older children. When the two little ones were old enough, they were sent to relatives in Louisville, Kentucky, with their two older sisters (Anne and Sarah). The children all received a good education. Peggy grieved at their absence but was cheered when letters from the four began to arrive. Her depression lifted over the years. When the children returned home in 1832, the family settled for four years in Fort Crawford. They lived in a two-storey wood frame house, where Peggy raised poultry, grew vegetables, and made dairy products for her family and the fort residents. She also perfected wine making that she would offer to visiting officials and other guests.

In 1835, their second daughter, Sarah, wished to marry Lieutenant Jefferson Davis, destined to become leader of the Confederate Army. Her parents opposed the marriage, not wishing their daughter to marry a soldier, knowing well the privations. However, when Peggy realised how much Sarah loved Davis she relented, though her father remained adamant. The couple were determined to marry, and they eloped. Their wedding infuriated Zachary even more, though he finally accepted the marriage. Three months after her wedding, Sarah wrote to her mother about her happiness and told her that she was visiting relatives of her husband. During the visit, she contracted malaria and died from the high fever within a few days, at the age of twenty-two. Peggy was shattered by the sudden tragedy, exacerbated by the fact that she had also contracted the fever, and her health deteriorated further as she became severely depressed. She treasured Sarah's last two letters to her and carried them with her for the rest of her life. She could not forgive Jefferson Davis for taking away their daughter, and neither she nor Zachary spoke to him for many years. Ultimately, the two men were reconciled during the Mexican War and Peggy made her peace with him during a chance meeting. They also met Jefferson and his second wife, Varina, many years later in the White House.

By 1836, the remaining children had left to pursue their own lives and Peggy became lonely once more. Her depression returned as her delicate health steadily worsened. In his concern for her, Zachary applied for long overdue leave, which was granted in 1837. For the first time in their married life, they were free to wander unbidden. They visited their daughters, Anne and Betty, who now lived in Philadelphia, and were also invited to meet President Van Buren in Washington. It was the first time that Zachary had entered the White House. Accompanied by Betty, their leisurely travelling continued, which brought a measure of peace to Peggy.

Inevitably, Zachary was recalled on account of the Seminole Indian battles. Peggy joined him in Tampa once the battles had been quelled. There she served as a nurse in the army hospital. In 1840, Zachary was posted to Baton Rouge, where Peggy spurned the spacious army accommodation provided for an army commander. Instead, she restored an old four-room cottage surrounded by trees overlooking the Mississippi. It was her first real home! She loved it. She planted a vegetable garden, built up a dairy, and taught other military wives to do the same. By then, her health had declined further, and she preferred to stay at home. She travelled on only two occasions when Zachary was stationed in Arkansas.

When Zachary was called to command the army in Rio Grande during the Mexican War, Peggy remained in Baton Rouge. She lived in daily terror that her husband would be killed in what was to become his most famous battle. Peggy became deeply religious and uncharacteristically used her status as the wife of a great war general as she rallied citizens to establish the Episcopalian Parish Church of St. James.

When New Orleans celebrated Zachary Taylor's victory with parades and tributes to his heroism, Peggy was at his side. In a surge of popular sentiment, he was nominated for president by the Whigs. He later won the election. Although Peggy attended the inauguration ceremony, she did not attend either the Inaugural Ball or the dinner hosted by the outgoing president, James Polk, on the eve of his departure. She was seriously fatigued and in poor health, and it soon became clear that the First Lady would not be attending official functions.

Peggy remained in the background in the White House, seeing only relatives and a few personal friends. She spent the majority of her time ensconced in her personal suite, leaving only to attend church. Occasionally, when she felt physically better, she would agree to meet others. One aristocratic woman from Natchez met her and later reported that she was "gentle" and "refined," which surprised the socialites. During the election campaign, Peggy had been referred to as "vulgar, ignorant, and coming from a poor family," none of which was true. One cartoonist portrayed her in the image of Rachel Jackson, smoking a long-stemmed pipe, a habit in which Peggy had never indulged. It was clear that

Zachary's opponents, who had not looked for accuracy, had tried to undermine him through his wife. Those who had attended the inauguration ceremony had seen a kind lady with gracious manners, but they had still allowed the untrue criticisms to circulate.

Their daughter, Betty, who had married her father's aide, Colonel William Wallace Bliss, undertook the First Lady duties. By then, the public was used to the wives of presidents taking a back seat and welcomed Zachary's bubbly daughter. Peggy and her daughter worked as a team. Betty presided over the public functions as the official hostess, while Peggy focussed on the maintenance of the household. She oversaw the servants' duties and supervised the gardens, kitchen, and dairy. She also undertook the full care of her husband's health, diet, and wardrobe.

Betty was a popular young woman, known to the public and the press as "Miss Betty." The press once dubbed her as a "rustic belle," possibly as a result of the inaccurate description of her mother. The tag was soon dropped when it became obvious that she was well educated and sophisticated. Betty had a dainty naturalness. It was first noticed at the Inaugural Ball where she made a notable impact. Following immediately behind the Russian minister's elegant wife, Betty made an equally refined impression in her simple white dress and a white flower hair decoration. Onlookers were delighted with her.

By March 1850, Peggy's poor health had intensified, and she finally relinquished all domestic duties to her daughter, apart from those directly affecting her husband. From then on, Betty Bliss took on a more mature persona. During one White House reception, she was seen to lead conversations with men of important rank with great humour and sensibility. The following day, the media praised her poise and demeanour. They referred to her as Mrs. William Bliss, daughter of the president. "Miss Betty" had grown up!

On July 4, 1850, Zachary was scheduled to preside at the laying of the cornerstone of the Washington Monument. Peggy felt too ill to attend, though Zachary had wished it. To the consternation of the crowds, Zachary collapsed on completion of the ceremony. It was feared that he had suffered a stroke, though some contended that gastroenteritis was the cause of his death a few days later, only sixteen months into his term of office. Peggy was horrified and spoke with bitterness as she recalled her first comments when his nomination had been announced. Heartbroken, she ordered no embalming or state funeral and left the White House immediately for a private burial in Louisville, Kentucky.

In increasingly poor health, Peggy went to live with her elder daughter, Anne. She later spent time with Betty and her husband, becoming almost reclusive. Her only known public appearance since her husband's death was at the wedding of her son, Dick, in 1851. Peggy never recovered from the shock and tragedy of losing her husband, and she survived Zachary by just over two years when she died on the 14th of August 1852. An Episcopalian service was held for her in New Orleans. Her remains were interred beside her husband in what later became known as the Zachary Taylor Cemetery in Jefferson County, Kentucky.

Betty's husband, William, had died just ten days prior to her mother's death on the 4th of August 1852. She married Philip Pendleton Dandridge in February 1858. To her regret, there were no children from either of her marriages. Until her death at the age of eighty-five, "Miss Betty" worked tirelessly to preserve the memory of her father, both as a great military man and as the twelfth president of the U.S.

First Lady from 1850-1853

Abigail Fillmore

March 13, 1798 - March 30, 1853

*"Mrs. Walsh called here on Monday and wished me to ask you to use
your influence for her cousin... I am already beset by office seekers"*

(letters to her husband)

Abigail Powers Fillmore

MARY FILLMORE

(daughter)

Abigail Powers Fillmore was the First Lady for less than three years, but she left a famous legacy. When she and her husband, Millard Fillmore, arrived at the White House in July 1850, following the sudden death of President Zachary Taylor, she was astonished at the dearth of books. As an avid reader from childhood with a large personal library, she decided to establish a library in the White House. Almost immediately she requested that the president seek funds from Congress to enable this.

Millard Fillmore and his wife had chosen a suitable room on the second floor and arranged with William L. Cripps to build five customised, tall bookshelves within the room, pending the outcome of Millard's application. Their initial request was refused, but after further prompting by Abigail, the funds were granted toward the end of the Fillmore presidency. The library was stocked with old and new books, including educational resources, reference books, and world maps. Abigail moved her harp and piano into the library, and the family and personal guests would often sit and converse while Abigail played. It was to become one of the most pleasant rooms within the building. Abigail has always been credited with the development of the White House Library, with an assumption that she played a part in choosing the books. There is no written indication that she did, however, and the view now is that she made only a few suggestions to Charles Lanman, an eminent librarian and author, who had been requested to stock the library.

Abigail, the daughter of Lemuel and Abigail (Newland) Powers, was born in March 1798, the youngest of seven children. A prominent Baptist minister in Stillwater, New York, her father had emigrated from Massachusetts ten years prior. Her mother was descended from Henry Leland, who had emigrated from England in the seventeenth century. When her father died in 1800, he left the family impoverished, and there was little help from the local community, possibly as a result of unfavourable rumours relating to his personal morality that were openly discussed following his death.

For eight years, Abigail's mother struggled to keep the family together. She had been a teacher and was able to educate her children. She also taught her daughters to sew and manage a household. Their father had left a large library of educational books, and Abigail, always an avid reader, took the greatest advantage of the facility. She taught herself math, government, history, philosophy, and geography under the guidance of her mother. The family struggled financially, but after eight long years of continuous stress, they moved in with relatives in the village of Sempronius (now Kellogsville) near Moravia, N.Y. Abigail's elder brother,

Cyrus, nineteen years her senior, had moved there several years before, and he had become the teacher at the local school within a double-log house, built on former Baptist church land. Later, Abigail's brother, David, succeeded as the teacher, followed by a cousin (Gershom Powers). After that, a person unconnected with their family took over the post, but in 1815, Abigail herself became mistress at the age of eighteen. She supplemented her full-time teaching post by tutoring in the New Hope Private Academy, as well as two daughters of a paternal uncle. Her professional reputation soon spread, and she was offered a post opening a private school in Broome County. She took up the offer but eventually returned to Sempronius.

Abigail first met Millard Fillmore at the New Hope Academy when she was nineteen years old. One winter day in 1818, she was sitting at her desk marking school papers when she noticed a shy-looking farmhand watching her. After motioning him to her desk, she enquired his name and what he wanted. "I am Millard Fillmore, and I want to learn things," he told her. It turned out that Fillmore was not a farmhand but a weaver's apprentice who had received only rudimentary frontier lessons. He had been an indentured servant in farming and accounting, a woodsman, and a weaver. With an acute awareness of his education deficiencies and a great thirst for knowledge, he had saved sufficient funds to allow him a term or two at the college. Intrigued and impressed by his ambition and determination, Abigail decided to help him. Millard was there for only a few months and proved to be a clever young man, quick to learn, taking on obscure subjects as well as the basics. Together, they learned new subjects, and eventually grew close. They fell in love and became engaged in 1819, though they were separated for three years when Millard's family moved 150 miles away. As neither could afford travelling costs nor the time to visit, they kept in touch by letter. As she waited for Millard, Abigail helped to establish a circulating library in the surrounding area of Sempronius.

While Abigail fretted at Millard's long absence, her family did not regret the separation. Her mother and siblings objected to the proposed match, feeling that the Fillmore family was beneath them socially. They took every opportunity to remind Abigail of her father's prominent Massachusetts family, but she resisted their appeals and married Millard Fillmore in February 1826, seven years after their engagement, at the home of her brother, Judge Powers of Moravia. She was an unprepossessing bride, except for her intelligent blue eyes, which oozed kindness. Her groom, who always acknowledged his wife's part in his law and political career, dearly loved her.

During their long engagement, Fillmore served an apprenticeship as a lawyer and was admitted to the Bar. After their marriage, the couple had moved to East Aurora, where Millard built a house and opened a law practice. Abigail continued to teach until their son (Millard) was born in 1828. Their daughter, Mary, was born in 1832. When Abigail's teaching career ended, she began to study French and continued her prolific reading and piano practise.

In 1829, Millard had a spell with the state legislature in Albany while Abigail remained in East Aurora with their son. She kept in touch with Millard through lengthy correspondence. She began to build their personal library, which would eventually consist of over four thousand volumes covering law, literature, poetry, and the classics. By 1830, the family moved to Buffalo, where Millard had opened a law practice. Millard and Abigail together established a lending library within the city. For the next few years, whenever Millard returned from his journeys, he would bring armfuls of books for Abigail to feast upon and put into their growing home library.

By 1833, Millard's political career had progressed, and he spent a short term as a congressman in Washington. From 1836 to 1842, Abigail lived in Washington with him, leaving her children with her sister, Mary, in New York. She was lonely in Washington and missed her children, though she made good use of her time by attending Congress sessions, listening to debates, and mingling within the political social circle. She preferred museums, art galleries, theatre, and concerts to the social whirl. Eventually, Abigail began to take serious interest in politics, often joining in conversations with Millard and his colleagues. On one occasion, a delegation asked her to speak at the dedication of a building in the nation's capital, but she refused. She knew that if she were seen accepting such invitations, it might not be good for Millard, as it was not usual for women to make public speeches.

The Fillmore family returned to Boston in 1842, where

Abigail suffered an accident, resulting in a badly broken ankle, which failed to heal. She was unable to walk or exercise properly, and her health deteriorated. Her ankle gradually improved, though she was house-bound for two years and had to use crutches. Although her walking improved, she was never free of pain again.

Millard was elected as state comptroller in 1847, and they moved to a fashionable boarding house in Albany. By 1848, Abigail's health had deteriorated further, and she was forced into a sedentary life. It was around that time that Millard was chosen as the vice-presidential candidate. Abigail had not been well enough to attend the inauguration ceremony for President Taylor, nor did she go to Washington as the wife of the vice president because Millard did not wish any unnecessary stress to be placed on his ailing wife. She was on holiday in New Jersey when, on July 9, 1850, she heard of the sudden death of Zachary Taylor and that her husband had become president of the United States.

At age fifty-two, Abigail found herself in a position she had never dreamt she would occupy. The public was more aware of the First Lady role by that time, and the press gave her more coverage than any of her predecessors. Abigail, never a fashionista, became increasingly aware that personal presentation was important, not only for her but for her husband. She hired a personal maid who also styled her hair, and a seamstress who made her clothes. Proud of her husband, Abigail did not wish to let him down, and in spite of her health, she continued the established social protocol. Eventually, the receptions and dinner parties became an ordeal for her because of her continual back and leg pains. The long-established New Year's Eve Reception, when she had to stand for hours receiving guests, was particularly agonising, but since she respected her husband's position as president, she did not overtly complain.

During their term in the White House, Millard and Abigail were often visited by their daughter, Mary, who attended a number of public events when her mother was too ill to do so. A highly educated girl who spoke four European languages, modest and pretty, she was unaffected by the importance of her family group and always appeared at ease when substituting for her mother at dinner tables. During her father's last few months in the White House, it became necessary, due to her mother's increasing frailty, to pass the hostess duties to Mary. Though not twenty, she carried out the duties in a mature manner, and her good looks and vivacity enhanced her work.

Meanwhile, in an effort to overcome her stressful pain, Abigail took an interest in popular culture, and she met some of the world's greatest singers and musicians, artists, and writers. Her intelligent, stimulating conversations at relevant events ensured her continuing popularity. On one occasion, she covertly broke the First Lady protocol by attending a concert featuring her favourite singer, Jenny Lind, alone.

Abigail held a strong belief in equal access to educational opportunities and showed great interest in prevention of abuse to people or animals. Surprisingly, for all her well-known intelligence, she took little interest in the rights of women. However, she was appalled at the flogging tradition in the U.S. Navy and spoke clearly against it. When President Fillmore signed the 1851 Naval Appropriation Bill on September 28, 1851, flogging as a form of punishment in the U.S. Navy was legally abolished. It has always been assumed that Abigail may have had a significant influence on the president over this issue. She also strongly opposed slavery, based on her own moral standards and religious culture. Her husband's biographer, William Elliot Griffis, suggests that Abigail warned the president that if he signed the "Fugitive Slave Law" (requiring the return of slaves to the South), he would not receive the Whig's nomination for the 1854 presidential election. Fillmore did sign it and was not nominated!

When the Fillmore family left the White House, Mary moved with her parents to their Buffalo home. There she helped her mother pack for an extensive tour of the American South. The trip was planned in an effort to ease the pressures of the past few years and to gain therapeutic advantage for Abigail's pains.

Just prior to the onset of this journey, the newly elected Franklin Pierce and his wife suffered a tragic blow when their only living child, Ben, age eleven, died in a rail accident. The distraught Jane Pierce asked Abigail if she would stand in for her at the inaugural ceremony. Deeply sorry for Mrs. Pierce, Abigail willingly accepted, in spite of the closeness of their Southern tour. Inauguration Day was cold and snowy, and Abigail became extremely chilled from exposure to these elements. Following the ceremony, she booked in at the Willard Hotel, where she developed a severe chest infection and where she stayed for three weeks. During that time, her health steadily declined, and she died there on 30 March 1853 of bronchial pneumonia. This was a cruel blow to Millard and the nation, as everyone had admired the gentle lady who had overcome pain and illness to become a highly respected First Lady. At that time, media protocol did not allow the names of women to be mentioned in their newspapers, but they made an exception for Abigail Fillmore, led by the National Intelligencer.

Millard was distraught and sank into depression. "For twenty-seven years, my entire married life, I was always greeted with a happy smile," he lamented. His beloved daughter, Mary, remained with him in Buffalo and agreed with him when he wanted to preserve something of Abigail's "for the children." He had the silver-mounted harness from her carriage (a present from New York friends when she became the First Lady) melted down, and the silver was used to fashion two plates, each inscribed with Abigail's name, one for each of his children. More tragedy was to follow when Mary died on July 26, 1854, of cholera. Devastated and lonely, Millard sought solace from politics once more.

He married Caroline Carmichael McIntosh, the widow of a prominent Albany businessman in 1860. Millard died in 1874 and was interred in West Lawn, Buffalo, next to Abigail and his daughter. Seven years later, Caroline died and was buried alongside Millard and his family.

First Lady from 1853 - 1857

Jane Pierce

March 12, 1806 - December 2, 1863

" Oh how I wish Franklin (Pierce) was out of political life! How much better it would be for him on every account.

Jane Means Appleton Pierce

ABBY KENT MEANS
(aunt and "unofficial" hostess)

People would often remark that Franklin Pierce and his wife made an odd couple. Pale and shy, Jane was a fragile, sensitive woman, weighted with the tragedy of losing all of her three sons, while Franklin was a hearty man, prone to a few drinks when one would do. Jane had never wanted her husband to be president and had fainted when she heard about the nomination. In fact, she never wanted him in politics, though he was a member of the House of Representatives when they married. She hated being in Washington and when Franklin was elevated to the U.S. Senate some years later, she did not take pleasure in the honour.

"How I wish he was out of political life! How much better it would be for him on every account" she had cried to one of his friends who had commented on how miserable she looked. Indeed, not only did Jane look miserable, but the White House itself always appeared as a dejected, joyless place during Franklin Pierce's tenure. Charles Mason, chief of the Patent Office, once wrote, "Everything in that mansion seems cold and cheerless. I have seen hundreds of log cabins which seemed to contain more happiness."

Jane Means Appleton, the third of six children, was born in Hampton, New Hampshire, in March 1806, and she and her siblings were brought up in a strict Calvinist household. Her father, James Appleton, was a Congregationalist minister who became president of Bowdoin College in 1807. Her mother, Elizabeth (Means) Appleton, was from a wealthy background in Amherst, where she took her family in 1819 following the death of her husband. Jane was thirteen years old at that time, and although she grieved for her father, she quickly adapted to the new life. She and her siblings received a thorough education in Amherst, where Jane showed an aptitude for her lessons, particularly literature, though her writing remained poor throughout her life. Nothing else is known about the family's early life.

Jane Appleton met Franklin Pierce in 1826, two years after his graduation from Bowdoin. Her family opposed their friendship. Her mother may have feared the difference between their temperaments, and the family disliked Pierce's affiliation with the Democrats. However, Jane was drawn to the cheerful, handsome lawyer and in the rush of young love overlooked his political ambitions. Opposition to the marriage remained so strong that they did not marry until November 1834, when she was twenty-eight.

They originally met in somewhat dramatic circumstances during a thunderstorm. Jane had been reading in a local library when she glanced out of a window and noticed a storm brewing. The storm broke with great force just as she hurried outside to get home. A loud crash of thunder sent the timid girl reeling into an old oak tree, where she crouched in terror as the thunder and lightning continued. Franklin Pierce had noticed the pale girl as she dashed from the library. When he saw her distress, he ran to her, concerned that she was in the worst possible position under a single tree in a thunderstorm. He caught the slight young girl up in his arms and ensured that she got home safely.

Immediately attracted by her slender figure, long chestnut hair, sad brown eyes, gentle face, and quiet nature, Franklin was devoted to Jane from that first meeting. Their first child was born in February 1836, but he died three days later. Jane was devastated, and her delicate constitution gave way to deep depression as she struggled to fulfil her obligations as the wife of a burgeoning politician. She was never able to come to terms with politics, which she found disquieting and intimidating. She felt the same way about living in Washington.

Frank Robert, their second son, was born in August 1839, and Benjamin was born twenty-one months later in April 1841. The birth of her two sons brought the peace she had sought for so long, but in spite of the joys of motherhood, Jane's depressions remained. She worried about the effect of Washington life on her sons and gave thought to moving herself and the boys away. The conflict of these thoughts and loyalty to her husband may have been a strong factor in her mental health problems. Franklin could see what was happening, and at the end of his Senate session in 1842, reluctantly relinquished his career. The family moved back to

Concord, and Jane was happy again until the death of her four-year-old son, Frank, who died of typhus fever the following year. Two-year-old Benjamin became the centre of her existence. Tied up as she was with her son, she did not realise fully her husband's deep sorrow at the loss of Frank, nor did she sense his restlessness. Despite his successful law practice, Franklin missed the excitement of Washington politics, and they drifted further apart.

With the outbreak of the Mexican War in 1846, Franklin volunteered for service, much to Jane's dismay. He received a commission as colonel, rising to the rank of brigadier by the time he returned, a local hero. For the next four years, Franklin, Jane, and Benjamin lived what were probably their happiest and most satisfying years. Jane's frailty improved as she watched her beloved Ben grow into a fine youngster. By then, Franklin had returned to local politics but did not show any indication of his former ambitions.

However, Franklin's proven political prowess and military fame had not been forgotten. As his political career progressed, the Democratic Party nominated him for president, causing his wife's "long faint." She was devastated at the prospect and Benjamin also expressed his concern, probably influenced by his mother. When Franklin took his wife away for a short break, Benjamin wrote to her saying that he hoped his father would not be elected as he would not like to live in Washington. Benjamin knew his mother prayed fervently each night for his defeat. His father eventually convinced them both that if he became president, his office would likely prove to be an asset for Ben's future success in life.

Franklin was elected in November 1852 and decided to take his family on a Christmas trip to Boston as a treat before he began preparations for his inauguration. On their return journey on January 6, 1853, their train derailed and their coach plunged down a fifteen-foot embankment. Having rescued Jane from the wreckage, Franklin began a feverish search for Benjamin but could not see him anywhere. Joined in the search by Jane and other helpers, they eventually found the lifeless body of their eleven-year-old son. His head had been crushed beneath a beam. Jane could not even scream, and the horror of that sight would haunt her forever. For the following weeks, she was cared for at the home of her sister, Mary Aiken.

The whole nation was shocked, and for a time, it was thought that the inauguration ceremony would be postponed. After much deliberation, however, it was finally agreed that it must take place as planned on March 4, 1853. Jane was unable to attend due to her grief, but she asked Abigail Fillmore, her predecessor, to stand in for her. Abigail was glad to do so in view of the circumstances. Jane joined her husband in the White House later that month, though she had not recovered from the shock of Benjamin's violent death or the sudden death of Abigail Fillmore, who had caught a bad cold during the inauguration ceremony. She felt that Abigail's illness and consequent death due to pneumonia had been her fault. Her depression deepened when she heard of another significant sudden death, that of Vice President William King.

Always solicitous of his wife's welfare, Franklin had engaged a New Hampshire couple to undertake the household management of the White House to relieve Jane. Franklin also arranged for her dear friend and aunt, Abby Kent Means, to act as her companion in the White House.

Abby undertook the First Lady's social duties and found them easy to perform, and she was able to spend long periods with her beloved friend. When Abby was unable to undertake a particular duty, Varina Howell Davis (the second wife of Jefferson Davis) officiated as did other cabinet wives. However, none of them, not even Abby Means, was considered to be the "official" hostess.

For the first two years of the presidency, Jane liked to assume some of the duties. She would entertain at small tea parties and receptions but avoided large events. Eventually her delicate health deteriorated under the strain of living in the White House, as did her mental health. Occasionally her mood would lift and she would involve herself in the politics of the day, even attending congressional debates, state dinners, and occasional presidential levees. Jane, with more of an abolitionist background than Franklin, persuaded the president to release Dr. Charles Robinson, an ardent abolitionist and Republican, who was detained in a Kansas prison because of his strong views. However, she showed little spirit at the social events, and to Washington society she was little more than "the invalid at the House." During this period, Jane would spend much of her time writing strange, heartbreaking letters to her dead son, pouring all her grief and love into them.

Jane was a strict Sabbatarian, and she asked the White

House staff and the families of diplomats to honour the Sabbath in church. Not everyone did, but many felt they should.

In spite of her melancholy, Jane did show interest in a number of decorative changes to the White House. She had a much-needed furnace installed, as well as a tile-covered bathroom with hot and cold water, and purchased an expensive new rug for the East Room, which she particularly liked because of the unusual flower design which somehow reminded her of her childhood. She also cherished a well-loved and handsome China set which her husband had bought for her at the 1853 New York World Fair.

Jane's health became even more fragile toward the end of Franklin's term of office. At the close of his term in 1857, they travelled to Andover, Massachusetts, to stay with Jane's sister, Mary. From there, Franklin left to settle accounts in New Hampshire, but upon his return, they set off on a sea voyage that was to last three years. President Buchanan had generously given them the use of a government ship, the USS Powhatan on which the couple sailed to the Caribbean, then Europe. The idea was to help Jane recover her mental and physical health. They returned home in 1860, and memories of the trip lifted her spirits for a while, though the depressive state had become chronic and she had also contracted tuberculosis. Memories of Benjamin eventually reasserted themselves in the home where he had once lived, and she began to relive the rail accident and the sight of his broken body. She took to carrying the child's Bible with her everywhere. Her main comforts appear to have been visits to her sister in

Andover. As Jane deteriorated, she withdrew more and more into a fantasy world shared with her dead children.

Jane Pierce died in 1863 of tuberculosis in Andover and was buried at the Old North Cemetery in Concord, New Hampshire, alongside her sons. Her social allegiances were revealed from the contents of her will, with bequests to the American Bible Society, the American Society of Foreign Missions, and the American Colonisation Society. The remainder of her estate was left to her husband. Franklin died six years later and was interred next to his beloved wife in the Concord cemetery.

First Lady from 1857 1861

Harriet Lane

May 9, 1830 - January 13, 1903

*Harriet Lane was the niece, not the wife,
of President James Buchanan, and officially
fulfilled the position of First Lady during his term of office*

Harriet Lane

(Niece and First Lady of President James Buchanan)

Welcomed eagerly by Washington society following the sad years of Jane Pierce, Harriet Lane quickly became a success as White House hostess during the presidency of her bachelor uncle, President James Buchanan.

She was the youngest and liveliest of six children. Her mother, Jane (Buchanan) Lane, and her father, Elliot Tole Lane, were relatively wealthy due to Elliot's work as a merchant for the Buchanan Stores in Mercerburg, Franklin County. When she was nine years old, Harriet was such a handful following her mother's death that her father placed her and her sister with a maternal uncle, Edward Y. Buchanan. Two years later, when her father died, Harriet asked if James, her favourite uncle, could become guardian to her and her sister. James accepted the responsibility with delight, for he adored the girls, in particular his mischievous romp of a niece, Harriet, though he made sure he showed no favouritism.

Two years later, James found that his political career

was taking up much of his time, and he sent the girls to a boarding school in Charleston, where Harriet proved to be a quick learner. However, she remained the mischievous girl James so adored, and whenever he could, he would bring his nieces to Washington, gradually introducing them to fashionable circles. This practice prompted a letter from one of the school directors, Mrs. Mary Merritt, that requested him not to invite Harriet to Washington, inferring that it was discipline rather than indulgence that the girl required. The next year, Buchanan enrolled the girls into the Visitation Convent in Georgetown. The nuns worked hard with Harriet, attempting in vain to teach her to play a harp, but the school succeeded in raising her awareness of charity and sympathy, which stood her in good stead for the future.

Buchanan had purchased a rambling estate, Wheatland, near Lancaster. When their school days had finished, Harriet chose to stay with her uncle James (whom she called "Nunks") when her sister moved to California. She was twenty by then, full of zest and fun, and the rooms of the stately mansion rang out with the laughter of young people. Harriet was vivacious, audacious, flirtatious, and very beautiful, and she attracted many friends. She had one special male friend, Henry Elliot Johnson, though it was never a serious relationship, as Harriet was far too busy enjoying herself to be tied to one person.

In 1854, Buchanan was appointed as minister to the Court of St. James in London, and he took Harriet with him. Queen Victoria extended the rank of an ambassador's wife to his niece, and she always called her "Dear Miss Lane."

Harriet became popular at this royal court, and there were many suitors who admired her beauty and long golden hair. She would flirt with the young men, privately referring to them as "pleasant but dreadfully troublesome."

When her sister died suddenly in 1855, Harriet returned home, devastated by the death of the person with whom she had shared so many experiences. Her grief was almost insurmountable, and when her uncle returned, he was concerned at her suffering and deterioration in health and spirit. He had been approached about the nomination for the presidency, and he discussed the possibility with her, though he no longer wanted it. Harriet's insistence that he should accept the nomination persuaded him to do so.

James Buchanan was elected into what would become a turbulent term of office with many tensions. Harriet, at twenty-seven years old, was the natural choice for First Lady, and she was a breath of fresh air to the socialites and diplomatic wives. Harriet hosted the official dinners and receptions with poise, charm, and discretion. She found that she had to work out seating arrangements with discreet care to ensure correct precedence was given to dignitaries and that political foes were kept apart,but as the North and South troubles escalated, so did the impossibility of her task.

Harriet used her position in the White House to promote social causes, one of which was the improvement of living conditions on Native American reservations. She would often invite musicians and artists to White House events, which were enthusiastically attended. Harriet certainly enlivened the White House scene and conducted the social seasons more brilliantly than they had been for a generation. Her personal popularity grew, even as her uncle's deteriorated. Her hairstyles and extravagant clothes were carefully studied and copied, and parents began to name their newborn daughters after her. A popular song, "Listen to the Mocking Bird," was dedicated to her.

In 1860, Edward Albert, the Prince of Wales, visited the White House. Harriet had met him in London, and his visit was her greatest social triumph. She entertained him for several days; having planned the dinners, receptions, dances, and tours well in advance. She played the English game of bowls and even won against him. Forty years later, he was to invite her to his coronation as King Edward VII.

Towards the end of Buchanan's inept term of office, the White House had become very gloomy. Social events had almost ceased as the North/South troubles flared, though Harriet insisted on carrying out the official White House activities, emphasising how guests should not "talk politics." As a strong Unionist, she showed an unusual display of temper if she found her Southern guests ignoring her pleas.

On leaving the White House, Buchanan returned to Wheatland with Harriet, who continued to care for her uncle and work on social causes. She also began to think about marriage, though she did not marry for another five years. She married her first favourite boyfriend, Henry Elliot Johnston, now a Baltimore banker. The marriage was extremely happy, especially following the birth of a son (James Buchanan) in

1866. Henry Elliot was born in 1868, a few months prior to the death of her uncle James.

Harriet received a healthy inheritance from "Nunks" that included Wheatland, where they spent their summer months. However, tragedy eventually overtook Harriet's peaceful life. In March 1881, her eldest son died suddenly. In order to distract his wife, Henry took her on a trip to Europe the following year. Their younger son died with the same devastating suddenness in October of that year. Two years later, Henry died, also suddenly, in May 1884.

Harriet became a widow at age fifty-four, and the sudden deaths of the four people she loved most brought out her true strength. She sold Wheatland and moved to Washington, where she had many friends, and devoted the remaining twenty years of her life to civic and charity work. She had three objectives, all of which helped to dissolve her sorrow and all of which she achieved: care for needy children, a memorial for her much maligned uncle, and to bring appreciation of fine arts to Washington.

Harriet began the building of a sizeable art collection, consisting mainly of European work, and bequeathed the collection to the nation in 1903 upon her death. As a result of this generous bequest, the Smithsonian Institute named her "The First Lady of the National Collection of Fine Arts." The collection is housed in the Fine Arts and Portrait galleries of the Smithsonian Institution in Washington.

Harriet also bequeathed a generous sum of money to the John Hopkins Hospital in Baltimore to endow a home for invalid children. This later became known as the Harriet Lane Outpatients Clinic, an outstanding paediatric facility for thousands of children today. Another bequest provided Congress with funds for the Meridian Hill monument to President Buchanan in Washington.

All are fitting memorials for the young woman who so ably presided over the first, and to date the only, full bachelor presidency. (The only other bachelor president was Grover Cleveland who was inaugurated in 1885. He married Frances Folsom on June 2, 1886.)

Harriet Lane is unique in another respect. She was honoured with the naming of a U.S. Revenue Cutter after her. The SS Harriet Lane was commissioned in 1857, transferred to the U.S. Navy in 1861, but captured and scuttled by the Confederate Navy in 1863. There have been two further cutters bearing the same name; one was commissioned in 1926 and decommissioned twenty years later, and another was commissioned in May 1984.

First Lady from March 1861 - April 1865

Mary Lincoln

December 13, 1818 - July 16, 1882

*"I do not belong to the public; my character is wholly domestic and
the public will have nothing to do with it."*

Mary Todd Lincoln

Mary Lincoln was the wife of the sixteenth president, Abraham Lincoln. She was ecstatic when Abraham Lincoln received the Republican nomination for president in May 1860, and when he was inaugurated in March 1861, she huffed and puffed proudly. Mary was convinced that between them they would provide a great service to the country as she dreamed of reducing tensions between the North and South and restoring national harmony. She never thought that the glory she so fondly dreamed of would turn to condemnation for her and her husband.

Within the first five months of the inauguration, Mary became the subject of vilification. "Vulgar, extravagant, vain, greedy and corrupt" were just a few of the jibes against her. The attacks on Mary were so vicious that the Chicago Tribune came to her defence. In August 1861, their editorial stated that "If Mrs. Lincoln was a prize-fighter, a foreign danseuse, or a condemned convict on the way to execution she could not be treated more indecently." Others suggested that no lady of the White House had ever been so maltreated by the press and that the sneers of sensible people and the making of comic papers about her were the national consequence.

Mary was born in Lexington, Kentucky, in December 1818. She was the daughter of prominent wealthy banker Robert Todd and Eliza (Parker) Todd. The Todds were Scottish pioneers in Kentucky, and they later became leaders in education and public affairs. Mary's mother had died in childbirth when Mary was nine years old. Her father married Betsy Humphries within a year, and she eventually gave birth to nine children. The second Mrs. Todd did not take kindly to her stepchildren. Her coldness, on top of the shock of their mother's death, created a sense of insecurity that followed Mary throughout her life. The children lived a rich life in their large Southern home where the household slaves were treated as beloved servants. Mary came to abhor slavery, just as her future husband had done.

Robert Todd ensured that his children attended the best schools. Mary attended the Academy of Dr. John Ward, an Episcopalian scholar, along with her sisters. She was an eager student of poetry, drama, and literature. At fourteen, she was enrolled at the Madame Victorie Mentelle School for Young Ladies where she learned French, the social graces, and other suitable ladylike subjects, followed by a further two years under Dr. Ward's tuition. Around that time, Mary's step-grandmother began to show a particular interest in Mary because of her academic skills, especially in French. As a result of this interest, Mary's skills in the language improved considerably and she was more able to accept her stepmother's continuing aloofness. By the time she was eighteen, Mary had matured into an attractive, engaging girl. She was comfortable when she met her father's friends, including a number of congressmen. Conversation with them improved her debating skills and general political knowledge.

When Mary was twenty, she moved to Springfield, Ohio, to live with her sister Elizabeth who was married to the second son of Ninian Edwards, a well-known former Illinois governor who had served from 1809–1818 and from 1926–1930. Mary blossomed into an articulate, witty, well-read young woman and was so full of confidence that she expected to shine wherever she went. She soon became the belle of Springfield with her blue eyes, light brown hair, and plump, womanly figure. With an affectionate and gregarious nature, Mary had a number of potential beaux. She did not show particular interest in any of them until her friend, Stephen Douglas, introduced her to the lanky, earnest Abraham Lincoln. From then on, she had time for no other. It was not surprising that the young Lincoln became smitten with his new jewel of a woman, in spite of her sporadic moody outbursts.

Lincoln was ten years Mary's senior. He was a lawyer and legislator, but when they announced their engagement, her brother-in-law's family did not approve. The family's derisory disapproval, together with Lincoln's awareness of his backwoods origin and mounting debts, convinced him that he could not make Mary happy. There were many rows throughout that turbulent period that resulted in Lincoln asking to be released from the engagement in January 1841. Mary did not heed his plea or her family's disdain, and the couple finally married on November 4, 1842. They had decided to marry on November 3, despite the Edwards' disapproval, and Abraham purchased a wedding band inscribed with the words "Love is Eternal" and arranged a wedding ceremony with Reverend Dresser. On the morning of November 3, Mary calmly announced their intention to her sister. Astounded but realising that they could not stop the wedding at that stage, the Edwards family quickly reorganised the wedding and a reception in their own home for the following day. The couple were married by the Reverend Dresser in front of thirty hastily invited relatives and friends in a charming ceremony. Mary wore a white muslin dress, but no veil or flowers in her hair. Two friends and her sister Elizabeth attended her.

The couple left the wedding reception for the Globe Tavern, where they lodged for a year and where their first son, Robert, was born in August 1843. Later, they purchased a house on the corner of Eighth and Jackson in Springfield and lived there until 1861. This house later became the Lincoln Home National Historic Site. During the years in Springfield, Mary attended the Presbyterian Church, where she made many friends and was considered as a kind, well-thought-of neighbour. She gave birth to three more boys named Edward, William, and Tad. Mary adored all of her children and indulged the boys to such an extent that she shocked their friends. When Edward died at three years old, Mary could not speak of him without weeping.

Lincoln was away from Springfield about six months of each year as he built up his successful law practice. He eventually became a circuit judge and nationally known politician. While Mary missed her husband, she accepted the separations and wanted him to achieve his political ambitions as much as he did. However, following an injury she had sustained during the birth of her third son, Mary's health was poor and she suffered frequent migraine headaches under the strain of housework and bringing up her children alone. Her loneliness led to hysterical outbursts when Lincoln returned home and rumours of Lincoln's unhappy home life circulated. The rumours may have been exaggerated as both Mary and Lincoln looked back on those years as their happiest.

When Lincoln became a congressman, his absences became longer. In an attempt to overcome inevitable loneliness, his family spent the winter of 1847–48 in Washington, living in a boarding house. There, Mary was exposed to the ways of the entrenched Washington elite and when the weather improved after a harsh winter, Mary and her boys returned with relief to Illinois.

Mary remained deeply in love with Lincoln, and she continued to support him throughout his long political campaigns. In 1860, she found that Stephen Douglas, one of her first Springfield friends, was an opponent in the presidential race. The election results were disputed, but Lincoln was finally inaugurated as president following one of the most bitterly fought presidential campaigns ever.

When she entered Washington for the first time as the

First Lady on the presidential train, Mary was without her husband. In what is known as the "Baltimore Plot," the president's aides feared assassination attempts by secessionists and Lincoln was forced into a position of donning a disguise and leaving the train prior to entering the Baltimore-Washington train station. This had a traumatic effect on Mary and her children, and she felt it to be an ill omen.

Mary noticed immediately a lack of warmth toward her family upon moving into the White House in March 1861. She heard rumours that the Washington society was unhappy that "outsiders from the mid-west" were there, and found that the White House and the role of First Lady was not what she had envisioned. The problems between the states curtailed any plans she had to become the social queen of Washington. She found herself organising the redecoration of several rooms instead, and in anticipation of her hoped-for dazzling entertainments, she purchased a 700-piece set of Dorflinger crystal as well as a complete set of Haviland china. Her extravagant spending had begun!

The Inaugural Ball and the first few White House receptions were boycotted. Of the few who attended, a number were impressed by the charm, grace, wit, and vivacity of the First Lady. However, Mary continued to be treated as an unwelcome interloper, which caused her distress. She had, perhaps, not fully realised the extreme popularity of her predecessor, Harriet Lane. Conceivably, if she had been less effusive and as quietly charming as Lane, her critics may not have been so outspoken. Mary's natural vivaciousness, high spirits, and energetic nature came to the fore, however, and she had no intention of staying in the background, in spite of diplomatic advice from her peers.

Whatever Mary did as First Lady, she appeared to be wrong in the eyes of others. She was hailed as "parsimonious" when she cut down the White House dinners because of the war crisis, but when she arranged entertainment in order to boost morale, she was labelled "callous." The Washingtonians criticised her clothes as extravagant and expressed shock at the sight of her low décolletage, and the overdecorous flower ornamentation in her hair. When her spending on necessary decorations in the well-worn White House exceeded the grant, there was a further flood of abuse. No matter what she did, Mary could not do it correctly. She began to receive so much hate mail that she requested the mail clerk to shield her from it. Her unhappiness at the adverse gossip made her short-tempered and outspoken towards her antagonists. She made no attempt to endear or defend herself against outlandish rumours and exaggerated shortcomings. A Mrs. H. C. Ingersoll of Springfield, Massachusetts, called upon Mary in the spring of 1864 to seek support for the Union cause. When Mrs. Ingersoll asked Mary about her response to the press, Mary replied, "It is no use to make any defence, all such effort would only make me a target. It seems hard that I should be maligned and I used to shed many bitter tears about it. But since I have known real sorrow since little Willie died, all these shafts have no power to wound me." Mrs. Ingersoll was astonished to find the First Lady so different from the press reports and was eager to let the public know about their kindly bereaved First Lady.

A report of the meeting was not recorded in the Springfield Republican until 7 June 1875.

Mary rarely spoke of the death of her eleven-year-old son, William, from typhoid fever in February 1862. William had been more like his father than either Robert or Tad, and his sudden death almost led to the mental collapse of the distraught Mary, who suffered convulsions and nightly visions of her dead son. She began séances in an effort to "reach her lost boy." Lincoln spoke bluntly to her on one occasion. He took her to her sitting-room window and pointed out a clearly visible large building. He advised his wife that she should try to control her grief or it would drive her mad and he would have to send her there. It was an establishment for mental patients.

Mary's confession of her sadness over William's death did not lessen the criticism against her, however. Her enemies felt she was lucky to have been with him when he died. They considered her more fortunate than those whose fathers, sons, and brothers had been shot dead on lonely battlefields. Their elder son, Robert, was also criticised for not being in uniform. Mary, fearful of losing her son, fought against him going into the army. Finally, Lincoln found a place for him on General Grant's staff, after which the criticism subsided.

Lincoln's election success had caused eleven Southern states to secede from the Union and Mary's Southern heritage became the focus of much hatred. While she had relatives who supported the Confederacy, her own devotion to the Union and opposition to slavery were equal to her husband's. She was a strong supporter of Charles Sumner, a radical Republican from Massachusetts, who continually argued for stronger action to end slavery. The public did not believe any of this, however, and wicked rumours continued that she was a Confederate spy secretly aiding the Southern cause as the war went on. No one appeared to notice or acknowledge the many hours she spent visiting numerous hospitals for Union soldiers around the capital. As the charges became more vociferous, Mary remained an easy target for those who resented that her brothers were "fighting for the enemy." Still, Mary had some defenders who spoke out for her. Benjamin Perley Poore, a Washington journalist, praised her "hospitality, charity, graceful deportment, goodness of heart." Noah Brooks berated the "gossipers and envious retailers of small slanders" and said, "Mrs. Lincoln is a true American woman and when we have said that we have said enough in praise of the best and truest lady in our beloved land."

President Lincoln stood staunchly by Mary throughout the personal attacks and vouched for her loyalty on numerous occasions. She also had a confidante of considerable therapeutic benefit to her. She talked over her troubles with her dressmaker, Elizabeth Kecky, a former slave.

Mary continued to carry out her hostess duties efficiently throughout the dreadful time, though her reputation for lavish spending escalated. One day, in an effort to forget her personal anguish, she went on a shopping trip, not realising that members of the press had followed her. They published comments on the following day about her "lavish spending on personal items," which fuelled more hatred. Infuriated at this lack of courtesy, Mary became even more volatile, which did nothing to enhance her reputation. It was during that time that her problems became even more acute as she employed mediums and spiritualists to help her "reach" her dead son, spending huge amounts of money which the Lincolns could not afford. Lincoln's aides and cabinet members were privately stating at that time that the First Lady was a liability and an overemotional, heavy spending "hell-cat."

The 1864 presidential election proved to be a terrible episode of hate directed at Mary Lincoln. There was assault on her taste in friends, and she was accused of courting "low" company. The press continued to attack her heavy spending and callousness, of failing to pay her family dentist's bills, and of being a vain, unpleasant, and coarse woman. Lincoln's opponents had a field day. They ended the campaign with an election pamphlet which said, "We only write this to show the ladies of the land that the re-election of old Abe must involve the installation of his wife to which we are certain they will object." Those attacks were not the only ones, nor the worst. Lincoln was re-elected in spite of the dirty campaign.

Following the collapse of the Confederacy in 1865 and the ending of the Civil War, there was great joy in the Lincoln household and Mary hoped that a period of national and personal peace would prevail. On the afternoon of April 14, 1865, three weeks into Lincoln's second term of office, they took a solitary drive around the city, simply enjoying being with each other. On what was to be their last drive together, they spoke of future trips to California and Europe and where they would settle after leaving the White House. They had plans that evening to visit the theatre to see My American Cousin. Mary had developed a headache during the drive and considered cancelling the trip, but Lincoln felt that they should go, particularly because General Grant and his wife would be their guests. The Grants cancelled at the last minute, and the Lincolns took along Major Henry and Mrs. Rathbone. President Lincoln and his wife were given a huge ovation on their arrival at the theatre. During the third act, John Wilkes Booth suddenly burst into their box and shot the president. Rathbone wrestled with Booth as Lincoln, bleeding heavily, slumped in his seat. Booth eventually freed himself and jumped from the box into the crowd below in an attempt to escape. Lincoln was mortally wounded and died the following day.

Mary did not recover from the traumatic experience for many weeks. She was too distraught to attend his public funeral. Elizabeth Keckly helped her to move out of the White House when she had sufficiently recovered. "What a change, Elizabeth," Mary said to her faithful confidante. "Did ever a woman have to suffer so much and experience so great a change? Had my poor husband never been president, he might be living today. All is over with me."

She returned to Illinois with Robert and Tad, very concerned about paying off the family debts. She might have felt that her days of slanderous smears were over, but in November of the following year, William H. Herndon, a former law colleague of Lincoln, stated during a public lecture that a woman named Ann Rutledge had been Lincoln's first and true love, and that he had mourned her early death for the rest of his life. Mary was humiliated at the public's willingness to accept a story she knew was untrue. Certainly, historians have been unable to prove the veracity of a romantic relationship, although there was a woman of that name who had died prematurely whom Lincoln had known, and whose death had saddened him. There is no proof of Herndon's assertions that the Lincoln's marriage was an unhappy one. It was certainly true that Mary and the president had disagreements, and Lincoln abhorred his wife's temper tantrums. There is also evidence that they had much in common, including their children, politics, poetry, classical literature, and joint ambitions, and that their affection and esteem for each other had grown over the years.

The Herndon assault was just one of the many burdens of her widowhood. Three years later, she was devastated when her former friend and confidante, Elizabeth Keckly, published her memoirs on her White House years with Mrs. Lincoln. Mary regarded the book as "a breach of a close friendship." In time, however, the book proved to be a valuable source of appreciation of Mary Lincoln and her loyalties, as well as her mental and physical health problems.

The delay in settling Lincoln's estate was also a cause of disturbance to Mary's peace of mind, as were the consequent pressures of creditors and fear of poverty. She appealed to Congress for financial support to alleviate some of her financial difficulties resulting from the assassination of her husband without success. The appeals brought her under attack once again for her apparent greed. She tried to raise funds to pay off creditors by selling her First Lady gowns and jewellery, again without success. Many thought this to be most irregular behaviour, and the Springfield Journal suggested that Mrs. Lincoln "should be pitied for all her strange acts."

Eventually, the estate was settled and creditors paid off, though Mary's obsession for reckless spending persisted in spite of her fear of poverty. Her elder son, Robert, a Chicago lawyer, became concerned about her sanity as both he and his wife did their best to care for her. The press remained quick to publish stories about her curious conduct. In an effort to escape from all the hate, Mary and Tad left for Europe in 1868 to wander across the continent. She continued to suffer violent headaches and was brooding all the while about her financial situation. She carried on pressuring Congress for appropriate aid as the widow of an assassinated president. In July 1870, her friend Charles Sumner not only supported her application but defended her passionately against all the charges made against her since she had left the White House. Shortly thereafter, Mary was granted three thousand dollars per annum. The amount was increased to five thousand dollars in 1882.

Mary and Tad returned home in 1871. Tad, by now a handsome 18 year old, suffered from a persistent bad cold for a few weeks following his return. His illness took a turn for the worse, and he died soon after reaching Chicago. Mary knew that she could never recover from such a severe blow as she suffered with the memory of her three dead sons. She cried out at Tad's funeral, "One by one I consigned my idolised ones to their resting place. There is nothing left for me but desolation."

Her bizarre moods returned, and she became certain that someone was trying to hurt her, which made her afraid to sleep. Her volatility became worse, and her heavy spending recurred. On one occasion, her only surviving son, Robert, had to prevent her leaving a hotel in a half-dressed condition. She turned on him and screamed hysterically in front of hotel staff and guests. In his mother's best interests, Robert applied to have her declared legally incompetent, and she was subsequently sent to a sanatorium specialising in nervous diseases. Although she was free to roam the house and gardens, she knew herself to be a virtual prisoner and rallied supportive friends to come to her aid by furnishing relevant facts in support of her sanity. The outcome was that Mary was released within three months and declared "restored to reason" and Robert was removed as executor. She never forgave Robert and his wife for having placed her in such an undignified position and did not speak to either of them for a long time.

Mary returned to France on her release. She spent four lonely years travelling the countryside. Finally, almost blind and suffering severe back trouble following a fall, she returned to live with her sister, Elizabeth Todd Edwards, at the Edwards ancestral home where she had first met Abraham. She struck up a close friendship with Edward Lewis Baker, the editor of the Illinois State Journal and husband of her niece, Julia. Baker's friendship meant a great deal to Mary. In time, she reached a tenuous reconciliation with her surviving son, Robert, though she spent most of her time inside the Edwards' home, rarely leaving it. It was there that Mary Lincoln suffered a stroke. She did not recover from the ensuing coma and died on July 16, 1882.

She was interred at the Oak Ridge Cemetery at the side of her husband. Mary had achieved at last her great dream of resting at his side again. She had once said, "When I lie at his side I shall be comforted."

First Lady from 1865 - 1869

Eliza Johnson

October 4, 1810 - January 15, 1876

"It's all very well for those who like it, but I do not like this public life at all"

Eliza McCardle Johnson

MARTHA PATTERSON (daughter)

MARY STOVER (daughter)

One afternoon in the early spring of 1868, Colonel William Crook, friend and bodyguard of President Andrew Johnson, rushed to the White House Library to be the first to give his friend the result of the president's three-month impeachment trial. Crook then ran upstairs to the First Lady's room and loudly declared, "He is acquitted. The president is acquitted." The frail First Lady struggled out of her armchair and tearfully took his hand. "Thank you, Crook," she said quietly, "thank you for coming to tell me." Raising her voice, she then cried, "I knew he'd be acquitted, I knew it," as tears from her sunken, sad eyes streamed down her pale face. Crook did not find it necessary to inform her that the result had been narrowly achieved by only one vote. The trial had followed when Johnson had removed Edwin Stanton as secretary of war, a violation of the existing Tenure of Office Act, and was the excuse for impeachment of this politically unpopular president.

Eliza Johnson and William Crook had infinite faith in Andrew Johnson, the seventeenth president. Both were aware of his volatile, stubborn temperament and deep sense of insecurity, but they also knew him as a man of absolute integrity. His personal slogan, "Tell it as it is or not at all," had often got Andrew into trouble, but Eliza's calming influence always soothed him whenever his temper threatened to get the better of him. All she had to do was lay her hand on his shoulder and say one word for him to calm down. "Andy!" she would say softly, in a disapproving tone.

Born in Greenville, Tennessee, in 1810, Eliza was the only child of a shoemaker who had believed in education and worked hard to send her to an Academy in Greenville, where she was quick to learn. After her father's death, she joined her mother in making colourful quilts and cloth sandals. She continued to read all types of books and journals avidly when time permitted.

The young Andrew Johnson arrived in Greenville in 1826, having travelled with his parents from the North Carolina mountains hoping for work as a tailor. The weary travellers, loaded with pots, pans, and other household items, were noticed by a group of young girls as they went down the street. One of the girls laughingly said that when the boy got his face washed, he would make a fine beau for some Greenville girl. Eliza McCardle had noticed the determined set of the boy's face and allegedly snapped back and asked her friends not to laugh. She joked that she herself might marry him one day. Eliza greeted the wanderers and set about finding them lodgings for the night. She knew of a possible vacancy for a tailoring apprentice and pointed Andrew toward it. Andrew and his family settled in the town, and eventually, he began courting Eliza. They were married on May 17, 1827.

Andrew and Eliza moved into a two-room house in Greenville, the front of which was used as a tailor's workshop and also as a temporary schoolroom, where Eliza helped her unschooled, shy husband to establish a tailoring business, building his confidence along the way. She also taught him reading, writing, and basic math each evening. Quick to learn, he made remarkable progress as his gregarious and sometimes aggressive personality developed.

During the early years of their marriage, Eliza gave birth to two boys (Charles and Robert) and two girls (Martha and Mary). The children brought great joy, though the boys would ultimately bring grief as they became hopelessly alcoholic. A fifth child, Andrew Junior, was born in 1852, when their eldest was twenty-four, and it was following that birth that Eliza's health began to fail. It was presumed that she suffered from consumption, a diagnosis that described many ailments in that era.

As Andrew's business prospered and his confidence expanded, his extrovert nature grew stronger. As a result of his makeshift schooling, he became more studious, and his interest in politics grew. Eliza persuaded him to join a local debating group which helped to improve his oratory skills. From then on, his interest and involvement in local politics rapidly increased, and he was eventually elected as an alderman and later became mayor of Greenville.

With Eliza's support and management skills, Andrew's business prospered and the family moved to a larger house in Greenville. He became financially successful and his political career progressed through a number of offices, including state representative, U.S. congressman, and governor of Tennessee. In 1858, Andrew became a U.S. senator. His work within the Senate took him away from Greenville for long periods while Eliza stayed at home managing the household and business affairs.

In March 1862, President Lincoln appointed Andrew as military governor of Tennessee. His pro-Union stand, however, had considerably reduced his popularity, and when Jefferson Davis imposed martial law in East Tennessee, all Unionists were given thirty-six hours to leave. Mrs. Johnson pleaded serious ill health and was allowed to stay, though the Confederates commandeered their home. She and eight-year-old Andrew Junior were forced to seek refuge with a nearby relative. Conditions deteriorated quickly, and in September, she applied for and was given permission to leave. Eliza and her son suffered an arduous journey across military lines from Greenville to Nashville, where they joined Andrew. The ordeal had serious consequences on Eliza's health, and she became frailer.

Adding to her sorrows, their elder son, Charles, was killed after falling from a horse while in a drunken stupor in 1863. A year later, her son-in-law, Daniel Stover, husband of her younger daughter Mary, died of consumption. Her second son, Robert, continued to cause severe distress as his alcoholism grew out of control. By then, Andrew had been elected as vice president and spent most of his time in Washington. To Eliza's relief, Andrew had concluded that there would be so few duties for her to undertake that she need not have to travel to Washington, so she stayed in Nashville. When the family heard the news of Abraham Lincoln's assassination, Eliza immediately feared for her husband's life as he was elevated to the presidency, with almost a full presidential term to fulfil.

Eliza became anxious about the role of First Lady so suddenly thrust upon her. She knew she was not healthy enough to run the White House adequately, and the pressure and excessive criticism placed upon her predecessor, Mary Lincoln, also bothered her. Aware that her husband's policies were already creating difficulties, Eliza felt that she would not be able to cope with similar criticism. In addition, she had been diagnosed with tuberculosis. The family discussed these issues thoroughly, and it was agreed that their daughter, Martha Patterson, would assume the general household duties at the White House, assisted by her widowed young sister, Mary Stover. Their son, Robert, aided his father in routine work, and Andrew Junior attended school in Washington.

The family were not able to move into the White House until Mary Lincoln had departed in August, as grief and consequent illness prevented her from doing so before then. When they did finally arrive, their private living quarters were severely stretched, as the Johnson family of thirteen (including two sons, Martha, her husband and four children, and Mary and her two sons) tried to settle down. Eliza and her daughters were appalled at the state of the mansion. It was in a shambles following the hordes of curious people who had tried to pay their respects to Lincoln's widow. Many items had been stolen, perhaps as souvenirs, chairs were broken, curtains had been torn, the carpets were dirty, and the walls were substantially finger marked. The situation was discussed in Congress and thirty thousand dollars were appropriated for renovation. Martha Patterson thought that was hardly enough though better than nothing as she set about refurbishing the house, achieving results that astonished everyone. One journal remarked that when the White House was opened for the winter season, the change was "apparent and marvellous, even to the dullest eyes." It seemed, however, that few knew the fresh face of the historic house was due to the tact, energy, and taste of the president's elder daughter. Martha had even acquired two Jersey cows, and they grazed within the White House grounds, ensuring there was fresh daily milk and butter for the occupants.

Andrew's private office was on the second floor opposite his wife's personal rooms where she spent the majority of her time sewing, reading, crocheting, and playing with her grandchildren, whom she adored. Occasionally, she would take meals with the family, though she generally preferred to eat alone. Refusing all requests for interviews, Eliza saw only her family and a few servants, including her husband's personal staff. She made a point of overseeing his wardrobe and ensured that he was served the food he liked. Eliza had planned the accessibility of her room to the president's office to enable regular conversations between them. She would provide sensible advice on moral issues when required, but she never involved herself in politics. She clipped articles from newspapers and magazines for her scrapbook and significant news reports which she felt would be of interest to Andrew. She read the daily newspapers avidly and regaled Andrew with all the favourable news when he visited before dinner, reserving the unfavourable news until his visit each morning after breakfast.

During Eliza's stay in the White House, she went downstairs on two occasions only. The first was when Queen Emma of Hawaii visited the U.S. during a world tour. The second occasion was for a Children's Ball held in honour of the president's sixtieth birthday. Eliza, who loved all children, enjoyed the highly successful event immensely as she sat on a chair of satin and ebony. She could not rise when the children were presented to her, but she explained by stating, "My dears, I am an invalid, you see." According to press reports the following day, that had been obvious.

Between them, Martha and Mary carried out the presidential hostess role with enthusiasm and efficiency. Both ladies were praised, Martha, in particular, for their gentle, reassuring demeanour, though the public never ceased to wonder about the "mythical" First Lady. There were many conjectures about her, and many longed to meet her, but never did. Eliza's health condition was never revealed, and perhaps the various misunderstandings about Mrs. Johnson may never have arisen if it had been. She certainly would have gained public sympathy. As it was, Congress and the public had nothing but admiration for the president's family and the way they conducted themselves within the White House, even as the president's unpopularity grew.

Public faith in Andrew Johnson first disintegrated when, as a Tennessee senator, he had insisted on touring his state to speak against secession. His life had been threatened during that time, and when he became president, he fought against the Republican's reconstruction policies, preferring his own. This began a "back-stabbing" process and a movement to oust him from office. There was considerable unpleasantness for many months as the House continued to disapprove his handling of the defeated South in the strongest possible terms. There was an attempt to impeach him which failed, though the Radical Republicans had overridden Johnson's veto over a contentious issue concerning former slaves. President Johnson was eventually charged with "high crimes and misdemeanours." The popular sisters, Martha and Mary, continued to carry out the White House hostess role with their usual zest during the impeachment trial, never allowing their discomfort and sorrow to show.

Ulysses Grant won the 1868 presidential election. Shortly before his inauguration, the Johnson family left Washington, leaving behind an immaculate White House largely due to Martha Patterson's efforts. Following the ignominy of the impeachment, it seemed everybody agreed that the Johnson family's behaviour had been impeccable. The house itself was said to have been kept in elegant order throughout the presidency and the whole Johnson family left the White House with a spotless reputation. It has not been recorded whether this public approval had appeased Andrew Johnson after the horrendous months of his impeachment.

The remaining years of Eliza's life were comparatively

peaceful. She and Andrew returned to their restored and enlarged house in Greenville, and Mary married again during the same year. The marriage brought Eliza some measure of consolation, though she continued to grieve for her elder son, Charles, and her concerns about Robert's alcoholism remained. Anxious to reinstate his credibility with the American public and not wishing to relinquish public life, Andrew ran for Congress twice but lost each time. Finally, in 1874, he was elected by the Tennessee legislature to the Senate, where his colleagues warmly greeted him. He died from a stroke within six months of the election.

Seven months later, Eliza died at Greenville on January 15, 1876, at the age of sixty-five. She had lived a full life dedicated to her husband and family, but because she had been out of the public eye, her achievements are often overlooked. A selfless woman who had so much early faith in an unlettered, undisciplined, volatile man, with the patience to teach him to read and write and help him build a successful business, as well as the courage to stimulate the political career of a future president, she does not deserve to remain in obscurity.

Phase Three

THE NEW WOMAN
AND THE GILDED AGE

Julia Dent Grant

Lucy Webb Hayes

Lucretia Rudolph Garfield

The Arthur Ladies

The Cleveland Ladies

The New Woman and The Gilded Age

Mark Twain referred to the time period of post-Civil War and post-Reconstruction eras of the late nineteenth century (1865-1901) as the "Gilded Age". Captains of industry and financiers took over the now quiescent country. There was splendour, elegance, and entertainment on a large scale. Powerful bankers sought attention from rich industrialists. There was hob-knobbing with high-ranking military and naval officers, diplomats, and influential newspaper editors. Fashionable people were sought everywhere, and royalty became almost a fanaticism. That was the America into which the New Woman stepped.

Much has been written about how Abigail Adams, Mary Lincoln, and others had tried to make more of their role as America's First Lady than the traditional image of the nation's leading wife, hostess, and fashionista. There was a sixty-year gap between Adams and Lincoln, during which time the role had trundled along, with some highlights but with no particular elevation. Indeed, until the end of the 1860s, there was even a danger that the role could disappear as many First

Ladies opted out, citing illness or infirmity.

Sarah Polk, Harriet Lane, and Mary Lincoln contributed by chance rather than intent to stop the rot, but when Julia Grant became First Lady in 1869, things began to look up. It is true that the old image still clung lightly to Julia, but she did not belong to the line of "invisible" sickly First Ladies who had inhabited the White House for almost forty years. Neither did she belong fully to the era of the "New Woman."

President Ulysses Grant's inauguration was one filled with hope as the country tried to put the Civil War, Abraham Lincoln's assassination, and Andrew Johnson's bungled administration behind it. The optimism of the new president and his wife spilled over into the great crowds who had gathered to welcome them.

The charismatic Ulysses Grant and his wife brought charm and engaging cheerfulness to the White House as they began their tenure with extravagant spending. The press had a lively time keeping up with the antics of their family, particularly as their youngest child, Jesse, had a tendency to gossip to reporters about the family. A number of entertaining stories were printed, to the delight of the public. Here at last were White House residents with the same family dynamics as everybody else. Julia's extravagance in refurbishing the White House was noted, but after the previous sombre years, the public accepted this happily, realizing that this attractive family was just what the nation needed. The nation itself had taken up the new "Gilded Age" and in such an atmosphere, Julia could hardly be censured for her display of gaudy additions to her new home. She was also profligate in her entertaining, serving dinners of twenty to thirty courses, always accompanied by French wines. The indulgent nation watched as the White House gradually disengaged itself from melancholy. The American people had needed the reassurance which Julia had unwittingly provided.

Julia was not a "New Woman" in the sense of education and intellect, but could be likened to that doyenne of society, Dolley Madison, and was almost as popular. When Ulysses eventually retired, they ventured on a round-the-world voyage, their reputation having preceded them everywhere. They were treated like reigning monarchs rather than a former president and his lady. They dined with English royalty and drank with English workingmen. They were banqueted and received honours and gifts throughout Europe and the Far East as governments competed for their company. It was a truly fitting end to a presidency that had brought America out of the gloom and into the "New World." Julia Grant had set a new stage for First Ladies.

Following the Grant administration, there was a progression to modernize and even divert the First Lady role from a purely social one to something more substantive. Though it had not yet been achieved everywhere, suffrage had gathered force and more women were carving out careers of their own, running organisations, speaking in public on political issues, often being referred to as the "new women." There was much promise in this title, and Lucy Hayes was one of the first to receive it.

The fact that such a highly intellectual First Lady resided at the White House provided an ideal opportunity for transformation, especially as the role of women in general was changing so much. Improved educational opportunities had produced a generation of women who did not necessarily wish to follow in their mother's footsteps and who married much later, if at all, as they began to realise that marriage was not their only option. In some states, women were allowed to practice law, and 1879 saw the first admittance of a woman to the United States Supreme Court. Much of the impetus for change had come out of the Civil War, when women had been encouraged to take their first step out of the home environment into a new world.

When she became the First Lady, Lucy's lack of pretension and formality within the White House was well accepted, and her thoughtfulness towards the staff introduced a new atmosphere. She became a favourite of the press as she worked hard overseeing large receptions, receiving numerous callers, and carrying out the traditional presidential social whirl. There were some who thought Lucy was dull, describing her as a tight-lipped moralizer over the temperance issue, but it was her lack of political achievement that caused most disappointment. This was not what everyone had expected from this astute, scholarly woman. Women who had made suffrage their primary concern tried to enlist her help, and she was encouraged by the press to drop the traditional role and add her powerful voice to a number of issues. She accepted none of these overtures and as the wife of the president, she was not prepared to push past the complex maze of protocol and common sense and become involved in quasi-political issues.

The constant requests for support from individuals, political or otherwise, created a conflict between representing the majority and supporting cultural idealists, and the role of First Lady became far more complicated than hitherto. The number of requests escalated during the years, signalling that the role was changing in the eyes of the public from that of the nation's hostess to advocate of the people.

Lucretia Garfield, wife of President James A. Garfield, was another academic who fitted her own ambitions around those of her husband. As a student, she had once written a strong thesis on the rights of women, and historians have noted from her diaries that she was a capable, alert, and feminist-minded woman, who had somehow come under the thumb of a boorish husband. He assumed that she would carry out the role of First Lady in the traditional manner. Surprisingly, Lucretia shared her husband's views on suffrage, though she frequently moderated his narrow-minded thinking on the subject of women's rights. Her letters and diaries indicate an intelligent, capable woman who had decided to put her husband's career before her own independence, albeit reluctantly. One can only grieve for the wasted academic life of this scholar.

On Garfield's death, Chester Arthur became president, with almost a whole term to serve. A widower, his daughter was too young to take on the First Lady role and neither of his sons was married. He arranged for his sister, Mary

McElroy, the wife of a religious minister, to act as his official hostess during the heavy social season. An efficient, educated woman, Mrs. McElroy was respected by all who met her, but she showed no signs of wanting to carry out any further duties or pass any opinion on political issues, and the presidency passed without any significant female influence.

When bachelor Grover Cleveland became president, he asked his erudite sister, Rose Cleveland, to become his White House hostess. Her intellect surpassed that of any previous First Lady, and her speeches on women's rights were legendary, but she eschewed her academic life to answer her brother's summons. The press welcomed the attractive woman, but did not highlight her intellectual achievements, concentrating more on her fashion than on her recently published dissertation. Perhaps their disappointment with Lucretia Garfield and Lucy Hayes as "new women" had dampened their expectations and enthusiasm for scholarly types.

Rose soon became bored with the social commitments of the White House, however, and was relieved when her brother married Frances Folsom, an erudite graduate of Wells College. Young and eager to please her husband, Frances ensured that the White House ran smoothly and that functions were elegant, but steadfastly refused to associate her name with the many requests she received to champion reforms. When Cleveland lost the 1888 election, the promise of the "New Woman" through Frances Cleveland would have to wait for another time.

As the first hundred years of the American presidency came to a close, the three potential "new women" of that era, Lucy Hayes, Lucretia Garfield, and Frances Cleveland had, perhaps wisely, maintained the role of the docile, though not always compliant, role of First Lady. In spite of the promise of the "New Woman," there had been little evolution in the First Lady role during these first hundred years, though the general conditions of daily life had slowly begun to improve with extraordinary improvements in education, post- and prenatal care, and infant mortality. The traditional stereotype of a passive, dependent woman was slowly diminishing, and womankind's prospects were far better than they had ever been as the twentieth century dawned.

Full suffrage did not occur until 1920, however, and while the National Organization for Women sought to overturn discriminatory laws on such issues as property, inheritance rights, employment and pay, comprehensive legal rights did not materialize until the middle of the twentieth century. However, that did not deter the First Ladies of the new century from their steady progression towards the Modern First Lady.

First Lady from 1869 - 1877

Julia Grant

January 26, 1826 - December 14 1902

"I became an enthusiastic politician"

Julia Dent Grant

Julia Grant was exhilarated as her husband read his inaugural address. He turned to his wife afterwards and said, "Now, my dear, I hope you are satisfied." She nodded happily and exulted in the Inaugural Ball that evening, even though it was disorganised and somewhat chaotic.

Julia looked forward to redecorating the White House which had been left immaculate though not decorated to her taste. Julia and her husband were both modest and unassuming, and Julia meant to be a success as the nation's hostess. It appeared that at last there would be a genuine First Lady, rather than a substitute, and Julia was welcomed as people clamoured to meet her.

Prior to Ulysses' election, the New York Tribune had described the potential First Lady as a "sunny, sweet woman, too unassuming to be a mark for criticism, too simple and kindly to make the mistakes which invite it." Julia had no intention of laying herself open to criticism and thoroughly enjoyed her role. She was a success from the start, and society and the general public admired her tremendously. Everyone wanted to gaze upon the wife of the president and shake her hand, and her well attended receptions were elegant. Even the poorest guests at her Drawing Room events were made welcome. It did not matter to Julia whether they were fashionably dressed or wearing a plain work-day frock. Benjamin Perley Poore, an observer of social events at the time, once wrote, "There are ladies from Paris in elegant attire and ladies from the interior in calico, ladies whose cheeks are tinged with rouge and others bronzed by outdoor work, ladies in diamonds and others in dollar jewellery, chambermaids elbow countesses, and all enjoy themselves."

Julia broke protocol when she invited wives of the cabinet to join her in receiving guests. On one occasion, Secretary of State Hamilton Fish was contemplating leaving the cabinet. Julia urged him to stay, citing her great need for his wife's help at functions. Julia Kean Fish was a good friend, and the president's wife was saved from many errors by her friend's discreet intervention.

Democratic America appeared to have developed a passion for all things royal after the war. That passion reached surprising proportions and a number of the Grant's glittering, successful dinners were for royalty. The public eagerly swallowed up press reports about such occasions. Guests included the third son of Queen Victoria, Prince Arthur, the third son of the Russian Czar, Grand Duke Alexis, and King Kalakaua of Hawaii. No one cared whether Kalakaua was the third, first, or last son. They were just pleased to have him there.

Ulysses was elected for a second term. The winter that year had been cold and dreary and on the night of the Inaugural Ball, it was colder than ever. Following her first chaotic ball, Julia was anxious to ensure that nothing would go wrong and she planned the ball meticulously. Some guests were unable to attend due to the weather, and many guests left early because of the cold. Those who stayed covered up their finery with scarves and wraps as they danced. One unfortunate lady who suffered from bronchitis collapsed and died on the dance floor. The memory of that terrible night dented Julia's composure for many months. She planned her daughter's wedding to Algernon Sartoris of England to cover every eventuality, even choosing the month it would be held to ensure clement weather.

The weeks leading up to the wedding on May 21, 1874, left the whole of Washington agog with anticipation. Two hundred guests had been invited; there were eight bridesmaids, lavish floral decorations, and an exhibition of expensive wedding presents. The day was warm and sunny, and the banquet boasted many delicious courses ending with a special dish, "Epigraphe la fleur de Nelly Grant." The dish had been specially commissioned by Julia and prepared personally by the White House chef. It was the most resplendent occasion the White House had seen. The success of the banquet made up for the disasters of Julia's Inaugural Balls.

Julia's early life had prepared her in some small way for her destiny in regard to taste and fashion. She was born in January 1826 at White Haven, a typical wealthy Missouri plantation near St. Louis. She was the fifth of eight children.

Her father was Colonel Frederick Dent, a descendent of an English immigrant. Her mother, Ellen, was the granddaughter of a British nonconformist, John Wrenshall. Wrenshall settled in Virginia in 1794 and later helped to establish Methodism in West Ohio.

Julia attended a log school together with her siblings until she was eleven, when she moved on to a St. Louis private school. She was a plain-faced girl with a slight squint, blessed with warmth and vitality, making her a popular figure as she sailed through St. Louis society. She grew fully confident with her exquisite social graces and good education. Her vivaciousness, constant smile, and merry laughter attracted many a young lad to her side, though she did not fall in love until she met Ulysses Grant.

Ulysses visited Julia's home at the invitation of her brother, Frederick, with whom he shared a room at the West Point military academy. He reminded Julia of the hero from her favourite book, The Dashing White Sergeant. Julia and Ulysses both loved horses and were expert riders, and they spent hours riding together, discussing books and horticulture. Entranced, he later told a friend that she was perfect for him. Some months later they sought approval from her father to become engaged. It was not granted. Colonel Dent did not believe that such a quiet young man with no inheritance prospects could make his daughter happy. He wanted more for Julia than the lonely life of a soldier's wife. Julia loved Ulysses deeply, however, and agreed to a secret engagement. Ulysses wanted no one else. A year after the secret engagement, Ulysses returned to see her father and told

Colonel Dent that he and Julia wished to marry and that they would do so no matter how long the marriage was prevented. Dent noticed a new strength and determination in the boy. He reluctantly agreed to a wedding with the stipulation that they should wait until the end of the Mexican War. Julia and Ulysses married in August 1848, four years after they met. Ulysses' parents disapproved of the Dent family being slave owners and did not attend the wedding. Their marriage was happy from the start as Julia accompanied her husband to military posts in Detroit, Sackets Harbour, and New York.

In 1852, Ulysses was ordered to the Pacific Coast where Julia could not follow, and she did not to see him for two years. She returned to White Haven with two-year-old Frederick. Ulysses Junior was born in Ohio in July of that year. Julia bore two more children, Ella (Nelly) in 1855 and Jesse Root in 1858. They were indulgent, devoted parents and grateful that they lost none of their children to early death, as so often occurred in those days. Nelly and her brothers were proud of their parents, as they were of them, and much has been written about the devoted Grant family.

Ulysses returned to White Haven in 1854, after having been encouraged to resign over the charge of insubordination. Colonel Dent gave them land on which to build a house and farm, which they named Hardscrabble. Due to the 1857 economic circumstances, the farm failed, as did White Haven. Years of poverty and frustration followed as Ulysses tried other jobs. All his attempts met with failure. Eventually, they moved to Galena, Illinois, where Ulysses worked in his father's leather shop as a clerk. Julia accepted the poverty bravely and managed the financial situation as best she could. She could not help feeling disappointed that her husband appeared destined to remain a leather clerk.

The Civil War changed everything for Julia and Ulysses and many other families. Experienced military officers were needed, and Ulysses was called back into the army. He was sent to lead a rebellious volunteer regiment in Illinois with orders to "lick them into shape." He relentlessly drilled the men for several weeks. He earned their hatred but eventually led them through several successful attacks on Confederate troops. He became known as a ruthless butcher as he progressed quickly through the ranks and was eventually promoted to the rank of brigadier general. He was both hated and revered by soldiers and politicians alike. Ulysses was defended at all times by President Lincoln, and, when he won the battle with the main Confederate army just south of Richmond in 1865, the Civil War was over. Ulysses became a national hero.

During that period, Julia had not been idle. She joined her husband as often as she could and tended the wounded and ill soldiers. She wrote letters to their loved ones, mended uniforms, helped in the kitchens, and narrowly escaped capture in December 1862 at Holly Springs.

Her memoirs later revealed an interfering side of her nature. On one occasion, when Ulysses refused a request from her to release an ailing Confederate whose wife had spoken to her, there were bitter tears and hours of sullen silence. Ulysses finally yielded. He told her, "I am sure I did wrong.

I have no doubt pardoned a bounty jumper who ought to have been hanged." In 1863, she visited him at his headquarters. Within minutes she was asking why his men were cutting a canal, which would surely not be needed. She felt that he should mass his troops and rush upon Vicksburg, which would be obliged to surrender. Ulysses laughed indulgently as he explained his strategy and why he could not go to Vicksburg at that time because it would risk the lives of his men. He explained that his "useless" canal was to provide the men with an occupation and a form of therapy to keep their minds on that job and nothing else. Julia saw the sense of his comments and willingly backed off.

As the war ended, the Grants' circumstances changed completely. Ulysses was plied with honours, gifts, and even a house in Galena. During the unsettled times following Lincoln's assassination and Johnson's impeachment, Ulysses rode the tide of popularity. Julia rejoiced in his success and fame. She had grown addicted to the adulation and power showered upon them both. It was not a surprise when Ulysses was nominated for president and won the election in 1868.

Julia was determined to create a comfortable home at the White House for Ulysses and her two younger children, Nelly, who was fourteen, and Jesse, who was eleven. The casual presence of her children, her father, and other relatives added to the homeliness and unconformity of the White House. Unused to great wealth and overawed with the glitter, they each indulged in tasteless ostentation, often making errors of judgement in decoration and dress. With the help of Julia Fish's sense of good taste, Julia quickly overcame that phase. She dressed in luxurious silk gowns and beautiful jewels. Her hairstyles were admired and copied, and her effervescence and joy of life ensured her and her husband's continued popularity.Their way of life seemed to embody the "Gilded Age" era, which was shared by many as America rejoiced in the comparitive tranquillity following the nation's turmoil.

In spite of loving their life in the White House, the Grants often felt the need for absolute privacy. They eventually purchased a holiday home at Long Beach, New Jersey, where they spent their summers.

Julia was an intelligent woman. She provided support and sometimes advice to her husband, although she never attempted to wield political influence. Ulysses was an astute president. One of his most famous achievements was the 15th Amendment. Ulysses, however, displayed a tendency to appoint incompetent and corrupt people, and Julia became involved unwittingly in the Black Friday controversy. There had been an attempt to jeopardise the gold market by unscrupulous staff. Ulysses had become aware of the plot in time to manage the situation and end the panic. However, it was later rumoured that Julia had been aware of the situation and had prewarned her brother-in-law, a financier, about it. Subsequent enquiries revealed her innocence, but the episode severely shocked her. She learned from that unpleasant interlude that she had to tread carefully to ensure her personal integrity.

Julia was happy in her role as First Lady and hoped for a third term and was excited and pleased when she heard of a possible third nomination. Ulysses was ready to retire, however, and early in 1875, he wrote to the press that he would not be standing again. Julia was devastated that he had not discussed his decision with her. He had known that had he done so, she would certainly have used her persuasive powers against his decision. She reluctantly left the White House in 1877.

Julia's compensation for her huge disappointment on leaving the White House was a two-year world trip. The couple had remained popular and were welcomed everywhere they went. They travelled to Europe, the Orient, and the Holy Land, and met and dined with many political leaders. Julia and Ulysses were guests of honour at a number of state banquets throughout their journey, including the court of Queen Victoria. Enthusiastic crowds followed them everywhere. Never, it seemed, had there been such a popular American couple.

The Grants returned to the U.S. in 1879 and settled in a town house on New York's Fifth Avenue. Ulysses became a silent partner in the Wall Street firm of Ferdinand Ward. It was discovered not long afterward that Ward had been stealing investments. His business collapsed and took with it most of Ulysses' personal wealth. The Grants personal reputation was also damaged, though there was no proof of their involvement in Ward's swindles. Ulysses had forfeited his military pensions when entering politics, and since there was no presidential pension at that time, they were once again in financial ruin.

The couple faced a second blow when Ulysses was diagnosed with terminal throat cancer shortly thereafter. He worried constantly about leaving his dear Julia financially unsupported and began to write his memoirs, knowing that their sale would support her. He found himself racing against time as his illness progressed. Wracked in pain, supported by pillows, he wrote every day and finished his work just days before his death on July 23, 1885.

Ulysses' friend, Mark Twain, edited the memoirs. They were a huge success. Their eventual sale enabled Julia to move back to Washington, where she lived the life of a grand dame, basking in the ongoing Grant popularity. The loss of her husband had a depressing effect upon her, though, that lasted a long time. Her new life in Washington helped her to recover as she cultivated friendships with future First Ladies Frances Cleveland, Caroline Harrison, and Edith Roosevelt. She attended events organised by the Grand Army of the Republic in honour of her husband, found comfort in the friendship of Varina Davis, widow of Jefferson Davis, and fully supported Susan B. Anthony and her suffragettes. Her melancholy disappeared completely when her daughter Nelly and three of her grandchildren moved in with her. Nelly had left for England following her glittering White House wedding in 1874 and did not return to the United States until 1893, when Congress granted her readmittance to American citizenship following the death of her English husband. She lived with her mother until the latter's death on December 14, 1902. Julia completed her own memoirs during that period.

They were not published until 1975 by the Southern Illinois University, seventy-three years after her death from bronchitis, kidney, and heart disease at the age of seventy-six.

In April 1897, the General Grant National Memorial, depicting mosaic scenes of his Vicksburg and Chattanooga victories, as well as Robert E. Lee's surrender, was dedicated with great pomp, ceremony, and parades. People from all over the world had donated over $600,000 to pay for the granite and marble mausoleum designed by John Duncan. Both Ulysses and Julia are interred there.

First Lady from 1877 - 1881

Lucy Hayes

August 28, 1831 - June 25 1889

"Woman's mind is as strong as man's ... equal in all things and is superior in some"

Lucy Webb Hayes

In 1877, journalist Mary Clemmer Ames described Lucy Hayes as the "First Lady of the Land." The press and public responded to the phrase which stuck to Lucy throughout the presidency and has remained in the nation's vocabulary ever since. The journalist's report had followed the inauguration ceremony of Rutherford Hayes, when readers of The Independent, a Protestant weekly newspaper, read that "Mrs. Hayes has a singularly gentle and winning face. It looks out from bands of smooth dark hair and there is a tender light in her eyes. I wonder what vanity will do for it." Mary Ames need not have been concerned that Lucy Hayes would change, for she was not one to have her head turned by attention and adulation. Her face remained natural, and her Methodist discipline never wavered.

The editor of the Philadelphia Times had often complained about the extravagance and pretentiousness of the "gilded age." He offered thanks, however, for Lucy's quiet dress sense. "She has carried into the White House the same dignity and ladylike simplicity for which she was so distinguished at home; her dress, invariably handsome and unostentatious, is becoming of the president's wife." Lucy's demeanour throughout her husband's presidency remained the same.

Under Lucy's influence, the Wesleyan White House became a place of daily prayers, Bible readings, and hymn singing. It was a million miles away from the grandeur of the previous administration. Wine was prohibited at state dinners which became very dull affairs, although the food remained of high standard. The secretary of state, William M. Evarts, pleaded with the president for wine to be served when plans for entertaining two Russian Grand Dukes were made in August 1877. He explained that a dinner without wine would be an annoyance, if not an affront, to the Russians. Both Rutherford and Lucy yielded and wine was served to the Russians, though that was to be the last time it would be served during their tenure.

Although it had been the president himself who had imposed the alcohol ban, his wife was nicknamed "Lemonade Lucy" as Methodists were inclined to give credit for the ban to Lucy. The Washington Temperance Society changed their name to the Lucy Hayes Temperance Society, even though she did not join any temperance societies and remained aloof of their activities. Her aloofness was a great disappointment to the movement. On one occasion, the president and his wife hosted guests on a river cruise. As Lucy directed her guests to a refreshment table, she committed her first and only indiscretion as First Lady. She led the guests to a table serving claret punch and said, "I want people to enjoy themselves in the manner that is most pleasing to them." The remark was overheard, and it was not long before it was reported to the press, and the Temperance Society quickly removed her name from the society's banner. However, Lucy remained on good terms with their officials and workers.

The first ever First Lady to have a college degree, Lucy's academic ability was well known. At that time, many assertive women were trying to find an equal place among men, and because it was known that Lucy had dabbled briefly with feminism at her college, it was presumed that she would symbolise the emerging "New Woman" in America. However, she refrained from taking up the cause of equal education for women, even declining an invitation from her school friend, Rachel Bodley. Bodley was the dean of the Women's Medical College of Philadelphia. Lucy and the president did visit Bodley's college at a later date, though Lucy preferred that her husband did most of the talking. She similarly turned down a request from Emily Edison Briggs to represent "American Womanhood" at the Paris International Exhibition in 1878.

The refusal of the intelligent and well-educated First Lady to become involved irked the rising businesswomen of the day. A Missouri woman wrote to Lucy that from her official position, she should take a greater interest in the development of women's industries than any other lady in the land. Emily Briggs was even more forthright in her criticism of Lucy. She said that American women had the right to know whether the president's wife approved of the progress of women in the high road of civilisation.

Although Lucy did not ignore those and similar comments, she preferred to keep her nose out of politics and remained detached. She took no part in debates concerning the admission of women to the Supreme Court, on which Rutherford finally approved a bill. Any suggestion that she had political influence over her husband was always refuted by her staff, though many continued to believe that in the absence of the president, Mrs. Hayes was the "acting" president.

Lucy was born in Chillicothe, Ohio, in August 1831 to a family that continually embraced new ideas and reforms. She was the only daughter of physician James Webb of Lexington and his wife Mary (Cook). Her father was totally opposed to slavery, and, when he inherited twenty slaves, he and his family returned to Lexington. He intended to make legal arrangements for the freedom and a new start for the slaves. When they arrived, Dr. Webb found himself caught up in a cholera outbreak and quickly returned his family to Chillicothe while he stayed behind to tend the sick. Unfortunately, he contracted the disease from which he died. His wife set about looking after her three children with limited funds. She refused to sell her husband's slaves, even though the money raised would have been helpful, and helped to complete the legal arrangements for their freedom. Their daughter, Lucy, inherited a hatred of slavery from her father that stayed with her all her life.

Her parents had always supported educational reforms and Mary Webb honoured their father's wishes that his children should receive the best possible education. Their schooling began at the Chillicothe Elementary School. Having invested her restricted funds wisely, Mary was able to move the family to Delaware when her sons were old enough to enter the Ohio Wesleyan University. Lucy also enrolled as their first female student and took preparatory and collegiate courses. In due course, the family moved to Cincinnati where the boys entered a medical school. Lucy attended the Wesleyan Female College, one of the few offering degrees to women, from where she graduated with honours in June 1850. It was there that she had taken a brief interest in the feminist movement. "It is acknowledged by most persons that a woman's mind is as strong as a man's. She is his equal in all things and is superior in some," she once wrote. As Lucy matured, however, she accepted most of the female conventions of the era.

When she was sixteen, Lucy met the young attorney, Rutherford Hayes. She was not particularly interested in him. Rutherford found the intelligent, lively young girl mildly engaging and told his mother that "she shows promise, but not quite old enough." His mother felt that Lucy would be a good wife for her ambitious son. She persuaded him to write to her, and they kept up an infrequent correspondence, which matured through the years. Rutherford wrote to his mother that "Youth is a defect which she is fast getting over and may be entirely out of her before I shall want her." Encouraged by the letter, Mrs. Hayes continued to manipulate her son into thinking that Lucy was the best person for him, and they teased each other about the prospect of Lucy as a daughter-in-law. "I need a wife to take care of my correspondence with friends and relatives. Women of education and sense always write good letters. I hope you will see to it that Lucy Webb is properly instructed in this particular," he once wrote to her. It makes one wonder what Lucy would have thought of this correspondence had she been aware of it.

Lucy and Rutherford met again in 1849 when Rutherford moved to Cincinnati and began to attend the college's Friday receptions. He wrote to his mother about their meeting and was soon expressing feelings of love. He spoke of her "low sweet voice," her "soft rich eyes," and of her intellect. He eventually wrote, "It is no use doubting or rolling it over in my thoughts. By George! I am in love with her." Fortunately, Lucy had grown to love him. They married in the Webb home on December 30, 1852, and were happy from the start, their marriage lasting for thirty-six years. They produced seven sons and one daughter, though three of the boys died in early infancy.

The couple always respected each other's ideals and aspirations, and when Rutherford defended a number of slaves in the law courts, he was probably influenced by his wife's strong opposition to slavery.

During the Civil War, Rutherford served as an officer in the Union Army where Lucy's older brother served as a surgeon. Whenever possible, Lucy visited her husband and her brother at the army camps, where she helped to nurse the sick and wounded soldiers. When she was unable to follow Rutherford, she visited local hospitals and offered help wherever possible. She corresponded regularly with her husband, who was wounded on two occasions. The first incident was minor, but the second was more serious. He faced the possibility of losing an arm. He received a musket wound in battle but did not stop, leading his men until he collapsed and had to be carried to the field hospital. Lucy's brother had saved the arm from amputation and arranged for an urgent telegram to be sent to Lucy. The telegram was held up and arrived late, but on receipt, she immediately left for the camp, leaving her children with relations. She rushed to the field hospital to find that he had been moved, though no one seemed to know where. It took two weeks of weary search and travelling before she finally found him ill and weak from his ordeal and worried about his family. Following a period of convalescence, they returned to Ohio by train.

Lucy's strength of character was tested during the journey. She and Rutherford had been allocated Pullman seats on the overloaded train because of his army rank. Seven disabled soldiers from Rutherford's regiment were on the train, relegated to standing space. Lucy was concerned at the plight of the men who had fought bravely for their country, and she led the soldiers to empty seats in the Pullman car, ignoring the disgust of "society travellers." Not long after the men were seated, Colonel Hayes was paged by a telegraph messenger and when the society folks realised with whom they were travelling, their scorn turned to smiles. Fruits, sweets, and other commodities were offered to the soldiers, but Lucy could not hide her contempt at the passengers who now basked in her husband's heroic reputation. As this story and a number of others became lore in the army camps, the

252 ■ Remembering the Ladies

soldiers referred to Lucy as "Mother Lucy." In spite of the devastating effect of the deaths of two of her sons during this period, she did not deter from her care of Rutherford and his troops as she quietly continued nursing, repairing uniforms, and listening to their troubles.

Rutherford's interest in politics continued throughout the war. In August 1864, he was nominated for Congress. He made it clear that while he accepted the nomination, he would not personally campaign, as he felt that an officer fit for duty in such critical times should not abandon the post to electioneer for Congress. He won the October election, probably as a result of his war record, sense of duty, and integrity, but did not resign from the army until May 1865 after the Southern surrender and Lincoln's assassination. It was then that he took up his seat in Congress.

Lucy spent time in Washington with Rutherford, which enabled her to practice her hostess skills. She entertained political visitors and friends in their rented home near the Capitol. While serving a second term in Congress, Rutherford was nominated by the Republican Party for governor of Ohio and during the election campaign, their longed for daughter, Frances, was born. When Rutherford was elected governor in November 1869, he focussed on state institutions and hospitals for the mentally ill and the deaf. It was during this period that Lucy took an active part in the formation of the Ohio Soldiers' and Sailors' Orphans' Home. She exerted extensive pressure to obtain institutional status. Rutherford chose not to run for a third term as governor, and, in 1873, the family moved to Fremont, Ohio, where they occupied a house built for them by Rutherford's benevolent uncle, Sardis Brichard. They named the home Spiegel Grove. In August of that year, when Lucy was forty-seven, their youngest son, Manning, was born. He died a few months later.

In 1875, the Republican Party leaders pleaded with Rutherford to stand for a further term as governor. He accepted and won an unprecedented third term. In 1876, he was nominated for president. During this campaign, wives of the candidates were scrutinised by the press. Lucy became a prime subject for inspection and gained a number of accolades. "Mrs. Hayes is a most attractive and lovable woman" wrote the New York Herald. Another newspaper wrote, "Mrs. Hayes is said to be a student of politics, able to discuss their changing phases with intelligence."

The race between Hayes and Samuel Tilden was so close that a special electoral commission was established to determine the outcome. It took many months to finalise, and it was not until March 2, 1877, that Rutherford Hayes was finally declared the nineteenth president of the U.S.

Rutherford and Lucy moved to the White House with three of their five surviving children; twenty-one-year old Webb, nine-year-old Fanny (Frances), and six-year-old Scott. Webb served as his father's personal secretary. Lucy was well liked by staff and visitors from the beginning. Although she disliked the formal dinners, she was a gracious hostess. She ensured quality food, appropriate seating arrangements, and the full comfort of her guests. Her reputation as the Lemonade Lady did not worry her. She accepted the title with good humour.

During their stay in the White House, Lucy installed bathrooms with running water and the first wall-mounted telephone. When an application for funds to renovate part of the White House was considerably delayed, Lucy personally searched the cellars and attics to locate and restore good but forgotten furniture. Thus, when the funding was finally granted, the consequent savings were spent on enlarging conservatories and building a greenhouse.

As First Lady, Lucy worked hard for benefits for war veterans, Native American welfare, and rehabilitation of the South, as well as for young people. She made frequent trips to the Gallaudet College for the deaf and mute and the Hampton Institute, where she sponsored scholarships and was a generous contributor to various Washington charities. One Easter, when children were banned from Easter egg rolling on the Capitol grounds, she invited them to use the White House lawn.

Rutherford had always intimated that he would serve only one term as president. In March 1881, he and his wife both thankfully returned to Spiegel Grove. Lucy became involved in local activities and joined the Women's Relief Corp in 1883. She also taught at the local Sunday school and worked for better prison conditions and improvements in the treatment and care of war veterans. She was persuaded to serve as the first national president of the Women's Home Missionary Society, and she sought the betterment for poor and destitute women. Her surviving children all become successful in their chosen work, and she was content.

Lucy died in her sleep following a massive stroke, at the age of fifty-seven on June 25, 1889. There was total mourning in Fremont on the day of her funeral, and she remains a well-loved memory, a symbol of the "New Woman" era. Rutherford died three years later. Both Lucy and Rutherford Hayes are interred in the grounds of Spiegel Grove, which was eventually deeded by their second son, Webb, to the state of Ohio in 1912, together with his father's library of 12,000 books. In 1916, Webb opened the first presidential library and museum in the United States.

First Lady from March 1881 - September 1881

Lucretta Garfied

April 19, 1832 - March 1920

"I'm going to try harder than ever before to be the best little wife possible"

Lucretia Rudolph Garfield

Lucretia Rudolph, nicknamed Crete, married James A. Garfield in 1858 following a strange courtship. History presents Garfield as a selfish sort of chap, full of his own importance, needs, and beliefs, hostile to the Women's Rights movement, especially their demands for the vote. He thought woman suffrage was atheistic and would result in the annihilation of marriage and family. Inexplicably, Crete, who was highly intelligent and well educated, accepted his views though in this modern era she might have snapped her fingers and sent him on his way.

When Crete became First Lady in 1881, many believed that she was even more cerebral than her predecessor, Lucy Hayes. She had jumped through many loops before then, however, and had slid from being a bright college student, who had written a brilliant thesis on women's rights, to increasing docility.

Crete was a shy, introvert girl who found it difficult to be the warm, passionate, and gregarious partner that James required. He had anguished over his feelings for her and certainly did not rush into marriage. He had discussed his lack of enthusiasm to marry her with his friend, who had reproved him for neglecting his fiancée. His friend cited the friendship that James had cultivated with Rebecca Selleck at his Williamsburg College. James told him in a huff that if he ever did marry, he expected to marry Lucretia Rudolph.

Crete was born in July 1831, the second daughter of Seb and Arabella Rudolph. Her parents were leading citizens of Hiram, Ohio, and devout members of the Disciples of Christ movement. Her staid parents never showed tactile affection to each other or their four children, but were passionate about education and insisted that the children attend school. All four attended the Georgia Seminary in Chesterfield, Ohio, where Crete's acquaintance with James Garfield began. Later, the girls went on to the Western Reserve Eclectic Institute (now Hiram College), founded by her father and the Disciples of Christ, which James also attended. The two struck up a tenuous friendship. After leaving Eclectic, Crete taught in Ravenna, Cleveland, while James went on to a prestigious college in Massachusetts. The two began a correspondence, initially about the study of dead languages. James grew increasingly attracted to Crete's considerable intellect.

James was a good-looking, charming young fellow with a number of women friends. His diary reveals his own wonderment as to why he continued his "written courtship" with the shy, serious Lucretia Rudolph. In the diary, James recorded notes about her lack of warmth, which he said he "needed to keep me happy." His gregarious nature needed love and affection which Crete did not know how to provide, and he was growing increasingly alarmed at her stance on women's rights. They were two disparate characters.

Their bizarre courtship continued in spite of doubts on both sides. Crete had become aware of his expectations, and she would write to him long, warm letters, to which James replied in a similar vein, each raising the expectancy of the other. When they met, however, they were strained and miserable. Crete spurned his affectionate hugs and kisses, even after they had become engaged. "When we meet," his diary noted, "there is no delirium of passion or overwhelming power of feeling that draws me to her."

Crete really loved James. She had never been able to tell him about the lack of tactile endearment in her home. Perhaps she did not realise that her childhood may have been the cause of her excessive reserve. On one occasion, James had decided to end the relationship, prompting her to show him her diary. Once he had written in his own diary, "I feel that under the proper circumstances I could love her, and unite my destiny to hers. With regard to her feelings upon it, I am not certain." On reading Crete's diary, he was overwhelmed, and there was no doubt of his feelings from then on. He wrote, "From that journal I read depths of affection that I had never before known that she possessed. My soul is full to over-flowing now." He returned to his college feeling great affection for her.

James's doubts returned when he met attractive and vivacious Rebecca Selleck, a fellow student with whom he spent much of his free time. Crete and Rebecca even met when they both attended his graduation oration. When he returned to Hiram to teach at Eclectic, he continued to correspond with Rebecca. At that point, Crete offered to release him from the engagement, which he rejected. He was not sure he wanted to lose her and asked her to give him time, which she agreed to.

Their wedding in November 1858 was held in her father's house. It was a cheerless occasion with only near relatives and a few friends present. They did not have a honeymoon and began their married life in a nearby boarding house, both continuing in their teaching posts.

James had become extremely serious about politics. In 1859, he was elected to the Ohio Senate. He left Crete at their new home in Hiram while he attended sessions in Columbus, and when the Civil War began, he was appointed as commanding officer of the Forty-second Ohio Volunteer Infantry. Immediately prior to that, he had told his wife that their marriage had been a "great mistake." Crete was not surprised, as she had heard of a casual romance he had had with a New York widow, Lucy Calhoun. However, she was devastated after having worked so hard to make things work between them. As her confidence declined, she had become submissive and docile. Her own intellectual thoughts and views were minimised to suit the wishes of her husband and the mood of the Victorian Era in which they lived. However, James soon regretted this outburst, perhaps because he had learned that he was to be considered for nomination to Congress.

1862 was the year of a "new beginning" for them. James had returned home a sick man after months of absence. Crete nursed him to improved health and on medical advice, arranged a period of recuperation and rest in a secluded farmhouse at Howland Springs. The time they spent there proved to be a turning point in their marriage. Crete and James enjoyed a kind of honeymoon at long last, finding that they really did care deeply for one another. Their first child, Harry August, who was destined to become president of his father's old college, was born soon afterwards.

It may have been a new beginning, but it took James a while to fully realise it. When he went to congressional sessions in Washington in 1863, he met the attractive Kate Chase, daughter of the treasury secretary, and began a liaison with her. Neither of them was romantically interested, and James even wrote to Crete about her, who gradually overcame any jealousy she might have felt. She was to feel more pain and jealousy, however, when he renewed his acquaintance with Rebecca Selleck. Crete wrote to James, "I should not blame my own heart if it lost all faith in you." He asked her forgiveness which, of course, she gave, and their new life continued.

On one of his home visits, Crete presented a tabulated paper to her husband. The document clearly indicated that in their five years of marriage he had spent a total of only twenty weeks with her. It shocked him, and they agreed that the situation should not continue. He took his family to Washington where, in due course, he built a house on Thirteenth Street, large enough for their growing family. They had produced seven children between the years 1860 to 1874, though their elder daughter Eliza died at the age of three years, and their younger son, born in 1874, survived for only two years. Their three older boys (Harry, James, and Irvin) eventually became lawyers, and each excelled as their careers progressed into the world of education and public service, while Abram, born in 1872, became a successful architect. Their only surviving daughter, Mollie, born in 1867, made a successful marriage with James Stanfield-Brow, who served as a junior White House secretary. In 1876, they purchased a farm in the town of Mentor, Ohio, which they named Lawnfield.

James spent a total of sixteen years in Congress, and became Speaker of the House in 1874. His nomination for president in June 1880 was the beginning of a strenuous period, but, when he won the election, he took with him a happy, cheerful family to the White House.

Crete was forty-nine when she became the First Lady, a slender, graceful woman, with clear, dark eyes and stylish brown hair. She was a handsome and popular hostess. She was not particularly interested in the social duties of the First Lady, but she undertook them conscientiously with genuine warmth and graciousness. There were few criticisms of her from the press, apart from her evident apathy. They were aware of Crete's formidable intellectual capacity and had hoped for headline-making statements from her. However, Crete had already made up her mind to deal firmly with what she thought were impertinent questions into her personal life. She had taken exception to early interviews when young journalists tried to obtain her personal views on matters of state, women's rights, the former president's ban on alcohol in the White House, and the presidency itself. They had left feeling that the First Lady had no personal views on anything of importance and made untoward assumptions about her in their columns. They were wrong, of course, but Crete was only too aware that any discrepancies between her views and those of the president would be scooped up into an unrealistic newspaper article. She felt she had reacted wisely to events that may have led to possible repercussions.

Crete had spent only a few weeks in the role of First Lady when she became ill with malaria and was sent to a New Jersey resort to recuperate. She was still there on July 4, 1881, when word came to her that her husband had been shot by Charles Guiteau in the Washington Railroad Station and was seriously wounded. Crete immediately returned to Washington, where she kept a vigil at her husband's bedside until his death in September, eighty days after the shooting. The cause of death was "serious wound infection," possibly caused as a result of physicians inserting infected fingers into the wound when removing the bullet. The whole country had monitored the president's condition as he fought for his life, and for once, the press was on Crete's side. The papers praised her stoicism as she helped to nurse and comfort him. Her grief, devotion, and courage during those terrible eighty days won her the respect of the country.

There was an outpouring of sympathy for Crete and her children. Pictures of the family were published throughout the country. The second assassination within twenty years was a severe blow to America. American citizens mourned

James in large numbers at many memorial services. Unsolicited monetary contributions to his family amounted to over $360,000.

Crete made history as the first presidential widow to participate in her husband's funeral. The widows of presidents Harrison, Taylor, and Lincoln, who all died in office, had not attended the ceremonies as they were deemed too trying for the widows. Crete assumed a prominent part in the funeral and ensured that the crowds would see her. She had felt that their grief was equal to hers and that she must demonstrate that she was of them.

Lucretia Garfield and her family returned to their Ohio farm, Lawnfield. The family received an annual income from a fund which had been established on their behalf from the $360,000 donations, together with a congressional grant of $50,000, and an annual congressional grant for presidential widows of $5,000. Thus, she was able to rear her family and live an active life without financial worries. Her children, each one an achiever, were her pride and joy. Crete became active in politics and participated in the Progressive movement. She had originally belonged to the Republican Party, but by the time of her death in 1918, she had switched to the Democrats.

Crete spent much of her time on her husband's papers, which she catalogued, carefully indexed, and stored. She eventually gave full access of the large collection to her husband's scholarly biographer, Theodore Clark Smith, thereby ensuring the factuality of a significant episode of American history.

Crete maintained her high intellect throughout her life. She survived James by thirty-six years and died of pneumonia in 1918 in South Pasadena, at the age of eighty-seven. She was interred in the Garfield Memorial in Lakeview Cemetery, Cleveland, Ohio.

Ellen Arthur

30 August 1837 - January 12, 1880

Ellen Arthur died in 1880, the year prior to her husband, Chester Arthur, becoming President.

Ellen Herndon Arthur

MARY McELROY

(President Arthur's sister)

Ellen Arthur was the centre of Chester Arthur's life and her wifely influence remained with him for the rest of his life, even after her untimely death two years prior to his presidency. Chester had married Ellen Lewis Herndon (Nell), a handsome woman, in 1859, and her death at the age of forty-two had devastated him and their two surviving children. She had been brought up to be a well-read, confident, elegant young woman, and was able to hold her own in the most aristocratic settings. She had outstanding social skills and conversational repartee and was once described as "one of the best specimens of Southern woman." Washington society would have liked and approved of this high-spirited woman.

Born in Culpeper in 1837. She was the only child of William Lewis Herndon and Frances Hansborough Herndon. Her father was a distinguished naval officer and one of the U.S. Navy's outstanding explorers and seamen, famous for his explorations of the Amazon. Her mother's uncle was Matthew Fontaine Maury, a reputed oceanographer. After being brought up in her father's hometown of Fredericksburg, she moved with her family to Washington, D.C., where she was confirmed in the Episcopal Church. As she matured, she moved with ease within Washington society. She would often visit her cousin, Debney Herndon, in New York, where she was to meet one of his roommates, Chester Arthur, in 1856. Nell, an amiable, vivacious Southerner of medium height with a slender figure, brown hair, and eyes, and spectacles that did not detract from her good looks, seemed an unlikely companion for Chester. He was a quiet, serious, rather staid lawyer, the son of a Baptist minister and a teacher, and seven years her senior. However, they fell deeply in love and saw each other as much as possible.

Nell's happiness was dashed a year later when her father went down with his ship, USS Central America, which had been caught in a hurricane off Cape Hatteras, in September 1857. The ship was heavily laden with many tons of gold valued at around $2 million, the loss of which contributed to the financial panic of 1857. Herndon was posthumously awarded a memorial column at the naval academy in Annapolis for having secured the safety of many of his passengers and crew, and the navy honoured his memory by naming two ships USS Herndon. Moved by his heroism, New York City provided his wife with a house, to which the family moved in 1858. Nell's mother was legally supported by Chester Arthur following the tragedy, assuring his full acceptance into the Southern family. The couple were married in October 1859 at the Calvary Episcopal Church and produced three children between 1860 and 1864, of which only two, Ellen and Chester, survived. .

At the onset of the Civil War, when Chester joined the Union Army, tensions plagued their marriage. The strains had begun prior to the war when Chester, a strong abolitionist, had won freedom for a group of Virginia slaves. Having grown up in the South, Nell's natural sympathies were with the Confederates, and her loyalties were severely stretched as she struggled to reconcile her Unionist husband's beliefs. Chester would often refer to Nell as "my little rebel wife" in company, which displeased her, as she was trying so hard to be loyal to him. When her husband became the Quartermaster General of the New York troops and was responsible for supervising Union Army supplies he found that his own loyalties were torn as he tried to assist his Southern relatives discreetly wherever he could without jeopardising his loyalty to the Union Army. On one occasion, during an inspection visit to Fredericksburg, he organised a few comforts for the Herndon family as they lived a precarious existence in the war-damaged area. Chester and Nell were grateful that Mrs. Herndon had moved to France, out of danger.

At the end of the war, Nell felt greatly relieved that Chester returned a fit and able man, and they rejoiced that their marriage had survived the many tensions. His law practice became successful over the years, and Chester and Nell were finally able to lead the kind of life to which they had always aspired. They eventually moved to a two-storey house in Lexington, purchased fine furniture, and acquired servants and tutors for their children. They became a part of upper-class society and dressed expensively in imported clothing. Nell became a celebrated hostess, adding sophistication to her dinner parties when she entertained her guests with songs in her wonderful contralto voice, a skill that earned them many a dinner invitation. Nell also sang at the Mendelssohn Glee Club.

Chester became interested in politics, resulting in his appointment as collector of the Port of New York, a post he held until 1878. As he became more affluent and influential, Chester slipped into a smoking, drinking, and talking habit, often leaving Nell lonely and neglected. The tensions in their marriage returned.

Early in 1879, Nell participated in a concert while Chester was at a political meeting in Albany. She caught a severe chill on that evening and quickly contracted pneumonia. When Chester heard the news, he rushed from Albany to New York, and arrived at her bedside minutes after she had slipped into a coma. She never recovered. He became a changed man from then on, and his grief and guilt regarding his neglect was forever with him.

Two years later, a still grieving Chester was appointed as vice president to President Garfield in 1881, and abruptly found himself the president of the U.S. when Garfield was assassinated a few months later. Chester longed for his wife at this time and felt lost without her at his side. Unable to forget her, he dedicated a stained glass window to her in the south transept of St. John's Episcopal Church where she had sung and where he was able to see it from his desk in the White House.

When Chester first saw the White House, he declared that he could not live in such a place for the next four years and arranged for famous New York designer, Louis Tiffany, to make changes. The president could be seen each evening checking on the progress, ensuring his standards were met, and declaring that he did not mind overseeing many of the details normally handled by a president's wife. This diligence did not, however, stretch to the hosting of receptions and dinners. When the redecoration was completed, he asked his youngest sister, Mary Arthur McElroy, to serve as the White House hostess and to supervise the education of his ten-year-old daughter. She made a positive impact on Washington society, and was well respected as she competently carried out the role.

Mary was the ninth and youngest child of William and Malvin (Stone) Arthur and had been educated at Emma Willard's Seminary. She married insurance man John Edward McElroy. There is sparse information about Mary's childhood and courtship, except that she was of pleasing appearance, with well coiffured hair, a pretty profile, and that she moved with grace and was quietly spoken. She and John produced four children, and her two youngest daughters often accompanied her to the White House.

Mary carried out the hostess duties with efficiency and decorum, though the president did not grant to his sister any formal recognition as First Lady. He had made it clear that he could not give anyone the place that would have been his wife's. This did not affect Mary's reputation, however, which grew as she presided over a number of important events. On occasion, she asked former First Ladies, Julia Tyler, Julia Grant and Harriet Lane, to help in receiving guests at the White House, and occasionally asked her daughters to assist. Fortunately for Mary, who needed to spend time with her own family within their own home, the duties were not too burdensome, as the social events had been restricted, in deference to the late President Garfield.

Mary's attentiveness and fulfilment of the role emphasised her commitment to the president and enhanced her personal reputation, even though, on occasions, she had to make unpopular decisions. For instance, she resisted pressure from temperance societies to ban alcohol from the White House and ensured that it was available at dinners and other social events.

Mary did not leave a lasting impression, just as her brother's administration failed to do, which ensured her disappearance into obscurity. One can only guess what Ellen Herndon Arthur, with her skills, talent, appearance, and vitality, might have contributed to her husband's presidency had she not died so unexpectedly. She would, no doubt, have been proud of her sister-in-law's maintenance of the presidential standards and the way she kept alive the spirit of the White House.

First Lady from 1885 - 1889

Frances Cleveland

July 21, 1864 - October 29, 1947

" I have not had a life yet, it is all before me..."

Frances Cleveland

ROSE "LIBBIE" CLEVELAND
(sister of President Cleveland))

Grover Cleveland was a lively forty-eight-year-old bachelor with a capacity for working long periods without a break when he was elected as president in 1884. As a result of his obvious good health and considerable charisma, he was the idol of many Washington matrons, who dreamed of him as their son-in-law. Mothers plotted as to how their daughters could meet him and knock him off his bachelor pedestal. If they did manage to meet this paragon, their dreams were soon dashed, as he efficiently, but charmingly, overcame their rapturous overtures. It appeared that he did not intend to marry, and when one of his sisters asked him about it, he said, "I have thought about it many times. The more I think of it, the more I think I'll not do it."

President Cleveland began his White House journey with his elder sister, Rose Elizabeth (Libbie), at his side. It was obvious from the beginning that Libbie was a natural, excellent, and most charming hostess, and Cleveland was proud of her. It seemed likely that she would successfully preside over the mansion for the next four years. Libbie was a learned lady and was welcomed by the Washington society. Their preference for more mature women had overtaken their earlier penchant for the youthful women who had dominated the White House for many years. Charming though somewhat formidable, with a Houghton degree, Libbie had already headed an institute in Indiana, studied several languages including Greek, and written a long thesis on the author and poet George Elliot. She was an established authority and advocate of women's rights, and she was noted for her temperance principles. Immediately prior to her White House role, she had been teaching in an exclusive girls' school. However, her main role in life, as she saw it, was the care of her mother and brother, so when Grover summoned her to Washington, she willingly put her career on hold. Her feminist ideas were a surprise to her brother, a traditionalist who believed strongly that a "good woman is one who loves her husband and her country with no desire to run either."

The press ignored Libbie's intellectual achievements and relegated the publication of her important George Elliot thesis to the inside pages, preferring, instead, to discuss her fashion and hairstyles. Libbie soon became bored with the White House social obligations, and it was often joked that when receiving guests she would be conjugating Greek verbs. She was perhaps relieved, as well as surprised, when she heard about the pending marriage of her brother. Soon after the wedding, Libbie returned to her own career. She edited a Chicago magazine for a while before taking up a teaching post in New York, and then she moved to Italy, where she stayed until her death in 1918.

Cleveland's wedding on June 2, 1886, was a source of amazement to the nation, though there had been some gossip about a "Folsom" romance. Oscar Folsom was an old friend and law practice partner who had died in a riding accident in 1875. His widow, Emma Folsom, had asked Grover Cleveland to administrate her husband's will and act as guardian to her eleven-year-old daughter, Frances. Grover, who had known Frances since she was born (he had even purchased her first baby carriage), agreed to both requests, ensuring her education was the best available. When she entered Wells College as a senior student, he asked Emma's permission to write to her daughter. Frances received many letters and flowers from Grover during the next two years.

Following her graduation from Wells, where she had excelled, Emma and Frances were invited to stay at the White House "to spend time with the president's sister." There was immediate public and press speculation, especially because they stayed for ten days. Was the president about to marry Emma, the widowed wife of his former business partner? No one had envisaged that it was Emma's twenty-one-year-old daughter to whom the president, twenty-seven years her senior, had proposed. They became secretly engaged, and, following the White House visit, Frances and her mother embarked on a trip to Paris, where France gathered together a trousseau. No novelist could have written a more enchanting love story. Frances tripped around Europe, loving her dear Grover (whom she had admired since her early teens), overcome with happiness. She was by then a handsome young lady with an air of confidence and the authority of a

much-older woman, the result of her Wells College education and of being the chosen bride of the president of the
United States.

Frances married Grover Cleveland in the Blue Room of
the White House on a lovely June day in 1886 in a glittering
ceremony. She presented as a sweet, shy bride as the proud
groom escorted his wonderful prize on his arm.

Once the public amazement of the president's secret
engagement and eventual wedding had calmed, the whole
nation accepted the news with joy. They felt they had been
given a gift of this accomplished, well-educated, handsome
First Lady, and if there had been speculation at the clandes-
tine courtship and age gap, it was quickly dispelled. The
couple clearly had a happy marriage following a properly
conducted romance, monitored at all times by her mother,
and as far as the bride and groom were concerned, the difference in age did not exist. The cloud of public disapproval
hanging over Grover following a rumor during his election
campaign that he had fathered an illegitimate child was lifted
and eventually forgotten.

Following a honeymoon in Deer Park, Maryland, they
returned to the White House where Frances at first appeared
reluctant to take on the duties of the First Lady. However,
as a new bride and with her willingness to do her best for
her husband, she tackled the job, taking advice when she
could. Frances became a success as the nation's hostess, and
won admiration from all as Grover and her mother looked
on proudly. Her luncheon and afternoon receptions were

friendly, chatty, and cheerful, and on one occasion, Frances had to receive a professional massage on her wrist due to the large number of hands she had shaken. The Chief Usher, "Ike" Hoover, appeared to worship the First Lady. "Her very presence throws an air of beauty on the surroundings, whatever the occasion or company," he once said.

The Saturday afternoon informal receptions Frances held were important to her and became a test of her strength. She had particularly requested these events so that women who worked during the week could attend. A Washington official approached her about them, urging her to discontinue them. When asked why, he expressed concern that half of the women attending were clerks and shop girls. He told the First Lady that "a rabble of shop girls" was not a suitable audience for her rank and that he was concerned for her dignity. Frances was indignant and argued that she had planned the Saturday receptions for the very purpose of allowing working women and busy mothers to attend a session denied them during weekdays. She informed the official with great firmness that under no circumstances would she refrain from holding the events. Furthermore, she gave specific orders that nothing must interfere with her Saturday receptions. Meanwhile, the Washingtonians, often a jealous, truculent crowd, accepted Frances with indulgence and affection.

Frances rejuvenated her staid husband and helped discourage his tendency to corpulence. Although he remained a workaholic, he became less lethargic with a new zest which eventually heightened the White House social occasions. While others found Grover difficult, Frances could placate him with ease, and while others found him impatient, especially if kept waiting, Frances would overcome this with a smile, a laugh, or a look. One afternoon they planned a drive together, and Grover completed his work quickly, eager to enjoy the occasion, and waited for Frances. She did not appear at the appointed time, and his impatience increased as her absence became prolonged. He took off his outdoor clothes in a huff. Finally, he heard her pleasant voice ringing out, "Come, dear, I'm ready now." Cleveland rose, ready to tell her off. He went out frowning, took one look at his wife, and his decision wavered for a second or two. "What do you think I did then?" he asked friends afterwards. "Why, I put on my coat and gloves again, and we went riding."

It seemed like everywhere Frances went, she was loved and admired. When the president and First Lady visited the West in 1887, the Ohio State Journal stated that there could be ten thousand men who could make as good a president as Cleveland, but that almost no one was better fitted to be a president's wife than Mrs. Cleveland. In spite of the social influence Frances had on Grover, no evidence appears to exist suggesting that she ever became involved in politics or that he even spoke to her about it. The young, inexperienced bride did not develop or show any interest whatsoever in that part of his life, preferring to be an adoring domestic wife and sparkling hostess.

Following four successful years as First Lady, the campaign for a second term began. Old rumors concerning an alleged illegitimate child resurfaced, and new ones began. Grover Cleveland was faced with slanderous accusations about physical cruelty and unkindness toward the First Lady. Appalled and angry at these allegations, Frances was driven to provide public testimony and evidence that she was a happily married woman.

The campaign ended by Grover winning the popular vote (many felt that this was due to the presence of his wife), but he lost the election. President Grover Cleveland left the White House exactly one hundred years after George Washington had been inaugurated as the first president of the United States of America. Frances, having felt that she was just getting into her stride as First Lady, was disappointed, but as she was escorted to her carriage by an old retainer, Jerry Smith, on March 4, 1889, she said to him, "Now, Jerry, I want you to take care of all the furniture and ornaments in the house, and not let any of them get lost or broken, for I want everything as it is when we come back." Somewhat taken aback, Jerry asked her just when she expected to come back so he could have everything ready. She replied, smiling, "Just four years from today." And they were!

The family of three, Grover, Frances, and two-year-old daughter, Ruth, was welcomed back by the staff four years later. They had spent the intervening four years quietly in their New York home, where Grover successfully practiced law and prepared for the presidential election of 1892, which he won. Ruth was born in October 1891, and two more children would be born during the second Cleveland presidency (1893–97). But that story is for another time!

Postscript

When First Lady Michelle Obama moved to the White House, she wasted no time in getting to know the real Washington. Not the guidebook Washington of famous buildings, monuments, museums, and posh restaurants, but the one which is cut off by the Anacostia River, an area mainly occupied by a Black population and where there is much unemployment and hopeless poverty. The First Lady appears acutely aware of other downtown areas within the city where the better-off and poor may live in close proximity but remain aloof, never integrating. Mrs. Obama's self-set mission is to change all that, and an ongoing "talking and listening" tour began early in her husband's presidency, taking in schools and centres for the homeless as well as those for the community and health care.

At schools, she sits down with students, teachers, and programme coordinators; at the homeless centres, she listens carefully and has been known to serve dinners; at the health centres, she will sit with health-care professionals and with patients. Cameras flash as she talks and listens, though this is not a publicity-seeking tour, but one where the First Lady requires an outcome. She has a dynamic, energetic team backing her efforts, professionals who realise the importance of the First Lady being seen as a role model for those wish to build on her objectives. With their help and support, Mrs. Obama is deliberately establishing a reputation for public involvement and compassion with every hand she shakes, every teacher, nurse, and doctor she thanks, every meal she serves, every tree or vegetable she plants with local children, every person she talks or listens to. She knows that she represents all the women of her country, and as her challenging aspiration to help the underprivileged overcome ill health, loss of dignity, and other deprivations continues, there is every chance that others throughout the land will be positively affected.

It is not surprising that with her empathetic social conscience, Michelle Obama, an intellectual high-achiever, might find it difficult to accept her main role as that of super-mum and fashion icon, attending pleasant social events and becoming a volunteer on politically acceptable projects. Like a number of her predecessors, she wishes for and needs more substance in her life, to work on a substantial campaign, though always aware that she cannot participate in the political world of the president.

There are examples of other modern First Ladies who found missions. Lady Bird Johnson championed environmental protection and beautification; Rosalynn Carter aided those with mental disabilities; Nancy Reagan of the "Just Say No" drug awareness campaign, and Laura Bush who sponsored childhood literacy. A number of First Ladies in the nineteenth century also took on ambitious projects. Harriet Lane worked hard to improve living conditions for Native Americans; Dolley Madison founded the Washington Female Orphans Asylum; Frances Cleveland helped to establish the Washington Home for Friendless Colored Girls, and in the early twentieth century, Ellen Wilson was the driving force behind the clearance of slums inhabited by poor African-Americans.

One of the differences between Michelle Obama's ambitions and that of her nineteenth-century predecessors is the strong professional team that backs her. One can speculate on changes which Abigail Adams, Sarah Polk, or Lucy Hayes might have achieved with such a team guiding them. Jane Pierce and Mary Lincoln may well have benefited from this type of support and guidance as they battled with their uncertainties and fantasies. Elizabeth Monroe, who could not stand the daily grind of visiting schedules resulting in upheaval within President Monroe's administration, may have found her role less onerous and easier to manage with such assistance, though in these modern times, her stance can be seen as a sensible development in the progression of an unfamiliar role. Indeed, the majority of the First Ladies within the first hundred years of the presidency might have reaped more satisfaction in their role with such support.

There are other differences between the nineteenth century and the modern era, the most significant being the attitude of men to women's equal legal rights and education, particularly in the first half of the 1800s. Poor pre- and postnatal care was another important factor, and, with the average number of pregnancies per marriage being eight, so was the sheer exhaustion of childbearing and motherhood. It was not surprising that together with a high infant mortality rate, the lives of many women were blighted with wretched physical or depressive conditions. Mental illness in the form of depression was a misunderstood sickness that often followed the birth or death of a child.

Modern women would not accept the restrictions placed upon the poorer women of the nineteenth century. From as early as six years old, girls from poor families were expected to grow food, spin cloth, and make household commodities. Most never learned to read or write, and opportunities to leave their environment were rare, so that the only respite in their narrow lives were parochial events and family relationships. Their menfolk had few prospects for a better life other than the army or navy, but the women had none at all, except an early marriage, childbearing, and a continuous life of drudgery. The personal fulfilment of women from wealthier backgrounds was not much different although life for them was easier, and there were opportunities for limited education and to change social status and environment through a good marriage.

The Revolutionary War helped to change this way of life. Men left the communities to fight, leaving women to run households, plantations, farms, and commercial enterprises, with consequent new challenges and opportunities. Women from all backgrounds became active in the war effort. Some refused to buy British products, while others formed groups to make shirts and uniforms for soldiers or raised money for the army. For the first time ever, women were able to make their own decisions and increase their political confidence as they fought in their own way for freedom, democracy, and a better life.

Samuel Slater, the Father of the American Industrial Revolution, brought manufacturing technology to the United States in 1789, which helped to transform America's economy and the lives of many rural women. Eventually, goods previously made by these women were mass-produced by Slater's workers, and the need to spin cloth in homesteads disappeared. Instead, the women were needed to work in the factories, providing an opportunity to leave home, broaden personal experiences, and save towards a more rewarding life. As the century progressed, the country moved from a rural-based society to urbanisation based on manufacturing.

Although circumstances altered, the same British rules about married women of any class persisted. Under these rules, women became part of a unit on marriage of which the prominent member was the husband. Women had no legal rights to their children or to buy and sell property, even that which they may have owned prior to the marriage. Abigail Adams had fought hard for equal rights for women, but her famous plea to her husband that he "should remember the ladies" was put aside as an irritation in the urgent task of preparing the Bill of Rights.

Education for women and girls during the first half of the nineteenth century was almost non-existent, with only the females from the wealthy plantation families learning to read, write, and perform basic math. Unless their families provided extra tuition, however, even these women were at a disadvantage in adulthood.

There was a breakthrough in women's education in 1742, when the Bethlehem Female Seminary (now Moravian College) was established. Within a year, it had enrolled over one hundred girls, but the fees were expensive and aspiring students from less well-off families could not afford them. The 1800s continued to witness significant changes in the growth of secondary schools and by the mid-century, women were being admitted to co-educational state colleges. Secondary schools were established for girls, which did not require students to stay for a stipulated amount of time or to undertake a stipulated curriculum.

An important change was pioneered by three women who individually led a movement toward the establishment of education for women which was equal to that of men. Frances Willard opened the Troy Female Seminary in New York in September 1814, Catherine Beecher founded the Hartford Female Seminary in Connecticut in 1823, and Mary Lyon opened a seminary in Mount Holyoke, Massachusetts, based on the Troy model in 1837. Similar establishments followed.

Education for all children from every background continued to improve following the Civil War, when more public funding became available, and the problems for women and girls due to a lack of education reduced significantly as the century progressed.

Just as education progressed, so did the world of medicine. In the nineteenth century, one in five babies died within the first year of birth, typically of a contagious disease, such as measles, diphtheria, tuberculosis, and pneumonia. Doctors began to study the impact of germs on health, and this work, together with the findings of Pasteur, Koch, and Soper, eventually led to immunisations and vaccinations against the common virulent diseases. Jenner had already produced the first scientific Smallpox vaccination as early as 1796. Research in New York had also revealed that one out of thirty-six people died from epidemics, attributed by scientists to filthy streets filled with horse manure as well as decomposing dead animals and vegetable matter. Successful efforts within New York to clean up the streets led to a spread of similar tactics nationwide, with consequent reductions in pestilence.

A concentrated effort to find the causes of infant and maternal deaths led to improved pre- and postnatal care and the publication of baby-care manuals. One of the most successful was written by L. Emmett Holt, a New York physician, who developed intricate models of cow's milk to resemble breast milk, leading eventually to a decreased mortality rate. By the end of the nineteenth century, many of the unfavourable health conditions had improved, though not completely eradicated.

The first hundred years of the American presidency saw all of these trials and tribulations, and as the century progressed, the era appeared to divide into three phases in regard to the First Lady role.

The first phase (1789 to 1829) lasted forty years, when it was clear that the first six American First Ladies were able to cope with most situations as a result of their life experiences and crises. They were from mainly well-off, educated backgrounds, with an in-built sense of loyalty towards the roles that they had undertaken. For the most part, these women complied with the unwritten rule of male dominance, even Abigail Adams, who was well used to having her thoughts and ideas acted upon. Between them, these six pioneers made an impact on the future role of First Ladies by creating a workable protocol, rejecting that which was clearly unviable.

The second phase (1829 to 1869) was much more complex. It was a stressful period, with political intrigue, treacherous scheming, a Civil War, and a seemingly remorseless group of elite socialites that threatened the demise of the First Lady role as a national symbol. Of the eleven presidencies during this strange era, the majority of the First Ladies found it convenient to appoint substitutes to carry out their role, pleading sickness or disability, which, in most cases, appeared genuine. A number of the legitimate First Ladies who relied on substitutes did, in fact, undertake the housekeeping aspects of the role and occasionally participated in the organisation of events, but it seemed that the socialites and the establishment preferred the fresh, youthful hostess who fulfilled the social aspects of the role.

It might be said that a number of First Ladies had opted out of their full traditional responsibilities because of the experiences suffered by the unfortunate Rachel Jackson and

Mary Lincoln. This can only be conjecture, though it is obvious that the period did little to develop the role of the First Lady. The public criticisms of presidential ladies of this era could be likened to that of some modern-day press reports, except that today's quality press presents well-researched criticism, while the nineteenth-century socialites tended to spread sensational gossip without stopping to think about its accuracy.

The third phase (1869 to 1889) incorporated the "Gilded Age," a phrase originated by Mark Twain, when the era triggered a welcome difference to the White House proceedings. First Lady Julia Grant was a refreshing change, a woman of verve and vivacity, reminiscent of Dolley Madison, though perhaps lacking her refinements and self-possession. After the sombre days of the previous administrations, Julia Grant's uncultured tastes and extrovert social behaviour created, for a time, an unimaginable sense of well-being within the nation.

In spite of the "Gilded Age" spirit, however, subtle changes were developing in the American psyche as the better educated and more informed populace began to look for increased stability. Had it not been for the "New Woman" era, the First Lady role could well have floundered, with a possible consequence that the White House could have been run by professional housekeepers and event organisers, with the First Lady's role no more than that of a consort. There is no suggestion that such discussions ever took place, but the role for the president's wife as envisaged by Martha Washington and her immediate successors appeared to have receded.

By the 1870s, women had begun to redirect their activities beyond that of their families, much of the momentum emanating from the Civil War. Hundreds of national women's clubs were organised that produced orators and thinkers with incredible influence. It was a time when the previous emphasis on youth was overtaken by admiration for women with good educational backgrounds, and Lucy Hayes, Lucretia Garfield, and Frances Cleveland were welcomed by both the public and the establishment.

By the time the erudite Lucy Hayes became the First Lady in 1877, there was encouragement from the public and the press for her to break out of her traditional role and become an advocate for women's causes. However, she continued to centre her life on her husband and family and rebuffed any attempt to draw her into feminist issues.

Lucretia Garfield took a similar stand, and although gracious in receiving those who sought her help, she gently eschewed the pleas, in spite of attempted persuasion from female relatives.

Frances Cleveland, the highly educated bride of President Cleveland, also took the view that her loyalty lay with her husband and his beliefs, and she maintained this stand during both of his presidential terms.

The public were disappointed with these women who had shown such promise for changing the role of women as a result of their academic achievement. They had not, however, taken into account the fact that these First Ladies had, in acknowledgment to their marriage vows, shown courage in their refusal to jeopardise their husband's presidency in any way.

So it was that by the end of the first hundred years of the American presidency, the role of First Ladies had not advanced as much as the achievements of politicians, scientists, educationalists, physicians, and the Women's Rights movement. What had been achieved, however, had made it possible for further tangible development which began with the inauguration of Theodore Roosevelt in 1901, when Edith Roosevelt became the First Lady. The new century would see dramatic changes.

Further Readings

I have read a number of the following books and have "dipped" into others. Also listed are a number of newspaper or journal articles that I discovered through the National Library of First Ladies in Canton, Ohio. I found this Library to be an essential resource for students of American presidential history.

The World Almanac of First Ladies

    (Lu An Paletta, World Almanac)

Notable American Women (Biographical Dictionary - three volumes)

    (Bellknapp Press, Harvard)

Modern Eloquence (Addresses and Tributes to Great Men)

    (Volume 5 (1923), Modern Eloquence Corp.)

Presidential Wives

>(Paul F. Boller,Jr., Oxford University Press)

"Dear First Lady"

>(Young, Dwight and Johnson, eds.,)

>(National Geographical Society, Washington, D.C. – 2008)

America's First Families

>(Carl Sferrazza Anthony)

American First Ladies

>(Roger James Sharp, Salem Press)

America's First Ladies

>(Chaffin, Lillie, Butwin, Lerner Publications)

An Imperfect God

>(Henry Wiencek, Farrar, Straus and Giroux)

Abigail Adams

>(Jane Sutcliffe, Lerner Publishing, Minneapolis)

Abigail Adams: A Biography

>(Phyllis Lee Levin, St. Martin's Press, New York)

Abigail Adams: A Revolutionary

    (Charles W. Akers, Pearson Education, New York)

"The Day Thomas Jefferson's World Fell Apart"

    (Robert Hay, USA Today, November 1989

First Ladies: A Biographical Dictionary

    (Dorothy and Carl Schneider, Checkmark Books, New York)

A Study of the Wives of the Early Presidents

    (Mary Ormsbee Whitton, Hastings House, New York)

75 Years of White House Gossip

    (Edna M. Colman, Doubleday, Page & Co. 1925)

America's Most Influential Ladies

    Carl Sferrazza Anthony, (Oliver Press, Minneapolis)

Dames and Daughters of the Young Republic

    Geraldine Brooks, N.Y. Crowell and Co. 1901)

As I Remember

    (Marian Gouverneur, D. Appleton, New York, 1911)

Autobiography of James Monroe
(Brown, Stuart, Gerry, ed., Syracuse University Press)

First Ladies, from Martha Washington to Barbara Bush
(Linda DeCesare, Random House, New York)

The Adams Women
Paul C. Nagel, Oxford University Press)

Andrew Jackson, His Life and Times
(H. W. Brands, Doubleday, New York)

"An Amiable Woman"
Katherine W. Cruse, Ladies Hermitage Ass., Nashville, Tennessee

"Andrew & Rachel Jackson"
(Peggy Robbins, American History Ill. 12.5–1977)

An Epoch and a Man
(Denis Tilden Lynch, Horace Liveright, Inc, New York)

Faith of the First Ladies
(Jerry & Marie MacGregor, Baker Books, Grand Rapids)

The Cooper Papers (7 vols)

(University of Alabama Press, Montgomery–1952)

And Tyler Too

(Robert Seager, Easton Press, Norwalk, Connecticut).

88 Years with Sarah Polk

(Claxton, Sparkman, Vantage Press, New York)

"Feisty First Ladies"

(Diane Cole, U.S. News & World Report, Jan. 30, 2006)

"Fillmore's Folios"

(New York Sun, August 17, 2004)

The First Ladies

(Sol Barzman, Cowles, New York)

Franklin Pierce, New Hampshire's Favorite Son

(Peter A. Wallner, Plaidswede Publishing, Concord, NH)

A Hell on Earth

(Michael J. C. Taylor, State University of New York Press)

"America's Bachelor President and the First Lady"

(Jack Elsen, Washington Post, September 22, 1984)

Harriet Lane

(Jill C. Wheeler, Abdo Publishing, Edina, MN)

Harriet Lane Johnston and the formation of the National Art Gallery

(Homer T. Rosenberger, Records of the Columbia Historical Society)

"Abraham and Mary Lincoln"

(Ruth Ashby, World Almanac Library)

"Abraham Lincoln's Widow"

(Mrs. H. C. Ingersoll, Springfield, Massachusetts Republican, June 7, 1875)

"Acts of Remembrance"

(Jennifer L. Bach, Journal of the Abraham Lincoln Association 25.2, 2004)

Andrew Johnson, President on Trial

(Milton Lomask, Octagon Books, New York)

Eliza Johnson, Unknown First Lady

(Jean Choate, Nova Publications, New York)

Civil War Wives

(Carole Berkin, Knopf Doubleday, New York)

The First Lady in Fashion

(Turrett, Bond Randle, Hastings House, New York)

The General's Lady

(Alice Fleming, Richard Leberson, Lippencott, Philadelphia)

The Administration of President Hayes

(John Burgess, Charles Scribner's Sons, New York)

Life of Lucy Webb Hayes

(Emily Geer, Kent State University Press)

The Garfield Orbit

(Margaret and Harry J. Leech, Harper & Row, New York)

A Quarter-Century of Machine Politics

(George F. Howe, Easton Press, Norwalk, CT)

"Everybody likes Mrs. Cleveland"

New York Times, January 22, 1880

"Frank" The Life of Frances Cleveland

(Annette Dunlop, State University Press, New York–2009)